Environmental Protection of the Himalaya

A MOUNTAINEERS VIEW

Environmental Protection of
THE HIMALAYA
A Mountaineers' View

Edited by
Aamir Ali

Published for
The Himalayan Club, Bombay

INDUS PUBLISHING COMPANY
NEW DELHI

© 1994, The Himalayan Club, Bombay

Published for
The Himalayan Club, Bombay
by Indus Publishing Company, New Delhi

ISBN 81-7387-012-8

Published by M.L. Gidwani, Indus Publishing Company
FS-5, Tagore Garden, New Delhi-110027, and printed at
Elegant Printers, Mayapuri Ind. Area, New Delhi

Contents

6

Preface

FINDING THE GOLDEN MEAN

The aims and objectives of the Himalayan Club are: 'To encourage and assist Himalayan travel and exploration, and to extend knowledge of the Himalaya and adjoining mountain ranges through science, art, literature and sport'. To fulfil this aim the *HJ* has endeavoured to cover a wide range of activities in the Himalayan range. However, mountaineering, climbing and explorations have received prime coverage, as they should, but over the years more space has been devoted to other subjects as well.

The *Himalayan Journal* now enters its 50th issue and as a celebration of the anniversary we are devoting this special publication to the environment in the Himalaya. Environment and its allied subjects is a vast field and a very specialised one too. Here we have tried to concentrate on how it relates to mountaineers on a practical footing. The impact of mountaineers on the areas in which they operate and the ways in which this impact can be minimised, is the subject of this collection.

We have tried to make this a postal symposium. Broad suggestions were sent to various members of the Club and leading authorities in this field. Their replies were edited and now form this book. The Club is fortunate to have Aamir Ali (Hon. Member) who agreed to act as the General Editor. His editorial knowledge, interest in the Himalaya and the environment and his ability to sift through vast quantities of material is unparalleled, the result of which is apparent for all to see. The Club and the editors of the Journal are enormously grateful to him.

There is a tendency to close the areas in the Himalaya once

they are threatened with any environmental or ecological damage. In the Himalayan countries the establishment of 'National Parks' means restriction and also, generally, closure. There is a hue and cry about cultural damage to the remote areas of the Himalaya which have recently been opened. The impact of tourism and mountaineering activity, in that order, are cited as culprits. Perhaps we mountaineers have been irresponsible. This book tries to give suggestions to change that anomaly. I feel that closure of an area for whatever reason is not a solution 'Prevention is better than cure'. A generation of mountaineers have grown up without enjoying the beauty of the Nanda Devi Sanctuary which has been closed for almost 15 years due to environmental damage caused in a decade of mountaineering. But is this the solution? That is the question one asks.

There is a growing concern, specially among mountaineers. Can you keep Ladakh, Nanda Devi Sanctuary and other areas as vast open air museums for the future by restricting access? What about the present generation. We only live once! The Alps have been enjoyed by millions with better protection than we seem to be able to provide. Why can't the same happen to the Himalyan ranges? As Aamir Ali wrote in one of his earlier articles 'Where is the golden mean by which the beauty can be enjoyed and as well be preserved?' This book tries to raise this question, study the problem and perhaps offer solutions. One hopes that it will lead towards 'the golden mean'.

HARISH KAPADIA
Editor
The Himalayan Journal

An Introduction

AAMIR ALI

To commemorate the 50th issue of the *Himalayan Journal* (*HJ*), the editor invited a number of leading personalities to take part in a Symposium on the Environmental Protection of the Himalaya: what are the main problems; what is being done to deal with garbage, toilets and fuel; and what practical action should be undertaken to prevent further degradation.

Contributions were received from George Band, Col. Ajit K. Dutt, Doug Scott, Michael Westmacott, Joss Lynam, Robert M. McConnell, Isobel Shaw, N.D. Jayal, Brig. D.K. Khullar (Retd), S.P. Godrej, Col. Balwant Sandhu, Kurt Diemberger, Manmohan Singh Bawa, Chris Bonington, Tony Streather, Sudhir Sahi, Capt. M.S. Kohli, Lindsay Griffin and Aspie Moddie.[1] The names are listed in the order in which contributions were received. Mingma Norbu Sherpa sent a description of the Sagarmatha Pollution Control Project, Sushil Gupta sent the Tentative Plan of the Gangotri Conservation Project and the Himalayan Adventure Trust of Japan sent a copy of the report on the International Symposium on Conservation of Mountain Environments, Tokyo, 1991.

Basic Problems

Several participants were quick to point out that the environmental problems of the Himalaya go far beyond garbage and human waste. Deforestation, over-population, over-grazing, poverty are the major problems. George Band and Joss Lynam both put

---

1. Unfortunately, the last three contributions were received too late to be taken into account in this covering note but it was possible to include their articles in the book.

deforestation at the top of their list. 'The Himalaya since the last two decades has been facing extreme pressure from the population explosion,' says Col. Dutt. 'The problems are various but all stem from the ever-increasing numbers of local residents, trekkers and climbers,' adds Mike Westmacott. 'The problem goes a long way beyond disposing of human waste and modern packaging,' says Doug Scott. 'Actually the rubbish and discarded equipment left on the mountain side is not of world-shattering importance. It is debatable as to how much the tourist has caused the deforestation on Himalayan hillsides.' Brig. Khullar says he has not 'touched the micro issues. These . . . are inconsequential and would be taken care of in case the economic miracle in the Himalaya can be ushered in.'

Manmohan Singh Bawa refers to the increase in *yatris* to the pilgrim centres; for instance at Hanuman Chatti, 'where during the *yatra* season one can see thousands of pilgrims squatting on the banks of the river and on both sides of the road itself.' Capt. Mohan Singh Kohli, Chairman of the Himalayan Environment Trust, stressed to the Tokyo Symposium, 'apart from the mountaineers and trekkers, the biggest problem is the pilgrim . . . (in 1991) we had over a million pilgrims going to the various Himalayan areas where shrines are located.' Sushil Gupta says that the Gangotri Basin, besides being visited by 75 mountaineering expeditions and nearly 25,000 trekkers, also receives '250,000 pilgrims annually. There are over 50 tons of rubbish lying on and around the trail leading to the source of the Ganges and beyond.'

'Deforestation is the worst feature of the modern changes,' said Joss Lynam. Robert McConnell viewed the 'major environmental problems . . . to be control of population and problems associated with the rising populations, including over-grazing by livestock and deforestation,' while N.D. Jayal points out that there 'is a tendency to look upon the environmental problems of the mountains as largely relating to the accumulation of garbage left by trekkers and mountaineers . . . However, a much more serious environmental problem in the fragile Himalaya concerns their limited carrying capacity in terms of the natural, productive life-supporting endowments of vegetation, soil and water.'

True, indeed, and no one would begin to dispute any of this. Just to reflect that the rivers flowing from the snowy reservoir of the Himalaya are essential for the survival of some half a billion people living in the plains below, is in itself a sobering thought. If the *HJ*, while asking for a discussion of the main problems of the Himalaya, set its main focus somewhat lower, on garbage, human waste and fuel, it is because these lie squarely within the orbit of the mountaineer; he cannot evade his responsibility for them nor claim that someone else must deal with them. These are problems that he creates and are within his power to solve; and it is his business to deal seriously with them. A wise old Indian poverb tells us that if we are too busy gazing at the stars, we will trip over the small stones under our feet.

Deforestation and Fuel

If deforestation is to be countered, there must be large scale afforestation; if the destruction of forests is to be stopped, there must be alternative sources of fuel available to the population. Certainly, mountaineers should not aggravate the problem by using firewood, however romantic, or allowing their porters to do so, however convenient.

While afforestation lies beyond the scope of most mountaineers, it is heartening to note that climbers have not ignored the problem and serious efforts have been made by some of them. George Band refers to the three nurseries for trees set up in Khumbu by the Sir Edmund Hillary Foundation. The one at Phurtse 'is producing some 30,000 three-year-old pine seedlings a year from seed for free distribution.' About a million seedlings have been planted since the Himalayan Trust began supporting this work 'but it is still only a drop in the ocean.' Doug Scott also refers to the New Zealanders who have planted huge areas of Khumbu with conifers. Isobel Shaw refers to three million trees planted every year in the northern areas of Pakistan.

N.D. Jayal has warned us against the predilection of Forest Departments to resort to monoculture—quick growing and revenue producing. S.P. Godrej rises in indignation against the 'plunder of the region . . . medicinal and aromatic herbs and plants which are nature's unique gifts at the height of 2500-3000 metres, are being systematically plundered by pharmaceutical houses of Bombay, Baroda and Delhi . . .' Perhaps we should remind ourselves of the three priorities set by the World Wide Fund for Nature (WWF): 1) biodiversity; 2) sustainable use of naturally renewable resources; and 3) minimizing environmental pollution and reducing the wasteful use of resources and energy.

Despite Nepal's National Conservation Strategy, 1988, and the National Environmental Policy and Action Plan published in August 1993, Nepal's forests continue to fight a losing battle against a population of 18.5 million growing at 2.1 per cent a year.

George Band stresses the need to encourage kerosene and camping gas. Col. Dutt says that he has been able 'to manage gas cylinders for all Himalayan Mountaineering Institute (HMI) courses . . . thus totally dispensing with the requirement for wood. The concept of gas has been spread and for the last three years I have used the platform of HIMTAB (Himalayan Tourism Advisory Board) to impress upon all the tour operators to switch over to gas for cooking and help us in protecting our trees.'

George Band notes with satisfaction that kerosene is being increasingly used in the Sagarmatha National Park and indiscriminate tree felling is banned. 'In 1978 we were among the first trekkers required to pay a small fee to enter the park. If a smart trader had set up at the entrance selling compulsory stoves and kerosene to trekking parties, he would be a millionaire by now!'

Tourism

It is of course mass tourism that has brought these problems to the forefront. Barely two generations ago, the Himalaya seemed a vast wilderness area, a natural heritage that would be preserved in pristine glory for ever; today we are all appalled at the degradation that we, inhabitants and visitors, have wrought in record time. Human beings seem to have an infinite capacity to be caught unawares by the problems that they do their utmost to create; thus it is with the Himalaya. Tourism meant money and therefore was to be encouraged with single-minded devotion; that this would degrade the attractions that drew the masses seemed to surprise us. And yet it is so with all the shrinking wilderness areas of the world as tourism grows exponentially. For example, while Antarctica received 4900 tourists in 1991, it is expected that in 1994 there will be 8000.

There are, no doubt, areas in the Himalaya which are still relatively untouched. After all, we are talking of a range that is 2500 km long and about 3.4 million km^2 in area, spread over eight countries, and home to 116 million people. But that can hardly be any justification for allowing the unimpeded destruction of any portion of this range. Environmental blight, like cancer, spreads.

'Tourism is the fastest growing industry,' says Isobel Shaw. 'The number of climbers, trekkers and mountain tourists increase. Is this increase sustainable from the point of view of the indigenous population and the visitor?' asks Doug Scott. He notes that there are over 200 trekking agencies in Kathmandu alone and the Government of Nepal is planning to increase tourists from 300,000 to 1 million a year by the end of the century. (Does the mind boggle?) 'The Nepalese Government has encouraged tourism without taking much account of its effect on the physical environment. It is time the carrying capacity of each area was worked out in a thoroughly scientific manner. For instance, did anyone at Head Office, on lifting restrictions, stop to consider where the 500-1000 people who may be at Everest Base Camp at any one time could evacuate their human waste there, and on the walk up?'

Well, of course not. The business of any Ministry of Tourism is to promote tourism; there may be other Ministries which are concerned with the environment but which will be way down in the pecking order and will generally wield little clout. They call for more expenditure; the tourist promoters promise more income.

George Band lists the overcrowding of popular peaks as a major problem, referring to the 19 expeditions to Everest in 1993 'with several hundred climbers and Sherpas milling around the Base Camp.' Isobel Shaw notes that in 1993, 77 expeditions were given mountaineering permits by Pakistan and 42 of these were for the Baltoro Glacier and Concordia. Doug Scott refers to sharing 'campsites like that in front of the Tengboche Monastery with anything up to 150 other people.' Sudhir Sahi estimates that 'in 1953, when Everest was first climbed, there were less than 12 expeditions and 100 trekkers. The position today (1991) is that there are approximately 300 mountaineering expeditions and over 100,000 trekkers every year.'

Chris Bonington urges expeditions to 'start planning ways of removing their rubbish from the mountain. Some of the more popular climbs on 8000 m peaks in particular, are an appalling mess because there has been no effort to take rubbish down . . . Dropping rubbish into crevasses is not a solution, since sooner or later it will be disgorged.'

Col. Sandhu refers to noise pollution and the number of agencies, settlements, building sites, shops and factories along pilgrim routes, despoiling a landscape that 'belongs to nobody.' And Manmohan Singh Bawa refers to river rafting, concentrated on particular stretches: 'The stretch between Manali and Bhuntar is a case in point. Hundreds of empty tin cans, polythene bags and other left-overs can be seen littering the banks of the Beas river.'

And now one reads that Myanmar is ready to jump on the tourist bandwagon and is opening up its end of the Himalaya to trekkers. It would certainly be unrealistic to hope that an adequate infrastructure would be installed before the invasion begins. Can anything be done so that it can benefit from the experience of other countries?

Bhutan is trying to restrict tourism to manageable proportions. By Royal decree, wrote Paul Sochaczewski of the WWF recently in the *International Herald Tribune*, 2 December 1993, 60 per cent of the land is kept under forest and hunting is banned in 20 per cent of the kingdom. Only 2500 foreign tourists are allowed in each year, says Doug Scott (4000, says Sochaczewski) and must pay $250 a day. Bhutan has launched a multi-million dollar plan to save its forests and to earmark large areas for total protection, but with a population of 1.4 million, growing at 2.4 per cent a year, it will be the familiar tug of war between people and forests.

Nepalese 'economic refugees' are coming in to Bhutan because the 'Nepalese have modified their traditional culture of Hinduism and Buddhism to accommodate a third religion, Mass Tourism,' says Sochaczewski. But Nepal has upped the rates for the popular peaks and 'increased fees should reduce the number of expeditions and encourage smaller parties to visit less crowded areas,' hopes George Band. (Which will then become more crowded?) Trevor Braham, a former editor of the *HJ*, writing about expeditions to Pakistan in the journal of the Swiss Alpine Club, *Les Alpes*, January 1994, said that the trend towards smaller expeditions of less than 6 people, seemed to be confirmed: 38 such groups in 1993 representing 64 per cent of expeditions against 23 per cent in 1992.

Should some areas be closed completely to tourism as S.P. Godrej and Sudhir Sahi suggest? In a recent interview published in *People and the Planet*, Vol. 2 No. 4, 1993, the President of the Nepal Heritage Society, Karna Sakya, a campaigner for 'sustainable tourism', said, 'If we want to develop tourism for tomorrow, we have to preserve some of the remote areas . . . Tourism can be disastrous. Take Lukla, near Mt. Everest . . . you will find a couple of thousand people. But when the tourist season opens more than ten thousand tourists go there . . . You can imagine the effect on this cultural and natural site. If we really want to save the natural patrimony . . . it is essential that we adopt the 'bed limit' system. It is probably not possible to adopt Edmund Hillary's idea of giving Everest a total rest for five years, but we could limit the number of tourists and increase the price of entering the area . . .'

It is encouraging to read that several reputable trekking agencies maintain very high standards, but it is inevitable that among the hundreds of agencies that have sprung up, there are many that are described by Col. Dutt as 'irresponsible . . . organized for commercial purposes,' and by Manmohan Singh Bawa as 'money grabbing tourist agents.' Doug Scott condemns unbridled free enterprise. *Les Alpes* has recently had several articles by Swiss trekkers who had had unhappy experiences with agencies: 'ripped-off' and charged for high altitude equipment for porters who never received any. One assumes that these agencies dealt with garbage and human waste in the same cavalier fashion.

The Trekking Director of a large Swiss agency made the same point to me the other day . He also said that a great deal depended on the local 'Sirdar' in charge of the porters. While many of the old hands showed a high degree of responsibility, this was not always the case with newcomers who were eager to cut corners and reduce costs and the general workload.

'Quality tourism' is the buzz word, says Doug Scott. Perhaps 'soft tourism' should also begin to buzz: where tourists are encouraged to stay with local inhabitants as paying guests, sharing their life and food. This brings income to the people without disrupting their traditional occupations. It is reported that local lodges providing food and shelter are increasing in Nepal.

Sociological Damage and Local Peoples

Several contributors refer to the sociological damage done to local communities by mass tourism—a phenomenon by no means restricted to the Himalaya, and a problem that seems intractable. 'The economies of Khumbu and Skardu-Askole areas have been revolutionised and turned into tourist economies,' says Joss Lynam. Manmohan Singh Bawa refers to 'the invisible and therefore more dangerous . . . pollution of indigenous culture.' 'Tourism encourages the commercialisation and distortion of local cultures. But cultures are bound to change anyway . . . In fact, tourism can preserve local culture in some form by showing interest in tradition,' writes Isobel Shaw. 'Cement is replacing the traditional style everywhere. The first priority in tourism development is to keep the area beautiful.'

The International Union for the Conservation of Nature (IUCN), in its Bulletin 1/94, reports encouraging news from Pakistan. In September 1993 the Government approved the designation of the Central Karakoram as a national park and has proposed to UNESCO that it be listed as a World Heritage Site. Jim Thorsell, IUCN's Senior Advisor, Natural Heritage, who carried out the feasibility study, noted that the most exceptional portion of the range was in Baltistan, with 60 peaks over 7000 m. 'The only problems on the horizon,' he said, 'are the area's growing use by trekkers and mountaineers, pollution of water supplies and depletion of fuel-wood. There are also signs that the social fabric of local communities is beginning to be disrupted.'

It is a self-evident truth that the local inhabitants must be brought into efforts of environmental protection. Joss Lynam feels that the local people must be educated and will prove the best environmental police. Mike Westmacott, referring to the degradation of the lower slopes due to wood cutting for building and fuel, believes that the 'key must ultimately be in the hands of local communities, more of which should be encouraged, or even compelled, to set limits to wood cutting, in their own long-term interest.' Brig. Khullar asks, 'How many of us have cared to ask the local people inhabiting the Himalaya as to what they think of it all and how best they can help the cause and themselves in the first place? . . . Let there be greater spread of education and health care and let the local economy get a real boost so that the people acquire the requisite motivation and pride in keeping their areas clean.' 'Self-help schemes are definitely the way forward,' says Doug Scott. 'Outside charity hand-outs can have a weakening effect on the local society.'

He also points out that the Sherpas themselves have cleaned up Sagarmatha with financial help from the WWF and have dug some 80 pits for rubbish. George Band tells us that the Sagarmatha Pollution Control Project is launching a public awareness and educational campaign. Chris Bonington stresses that this kind of local action 'seems by far the most effective.' The WWF also supported the Annapurna Conservation Area Project which, according to Doug Scott, 'has done such a fantastic job in the Annapurna region, especially with controlling the destruction of forests.'

Mingma Norbu Sherpa tells us that the Sagarmatha Pollution Control Project seeks to alleviate the problems of sanitation, trash disposal and deforestation. The Sagarmatha National Park covers 1243 km^2 and receives some 15,000 visitors a year. It is managed by the Sagarmatha Cooperative composed of members of the

National Park Service and the local Sherpa community, and is chaired by the Abbot of the Tengboche Monastery.

Isobel Shaw complains that 'most expeditions bring almost everything with them from their home country. This is expensive for the expedition and does not benefit the mountain people enough.' Joss Lynam reckons that 'in one of the best organized trekking areas, Annapurna, only about 10 per cent of the money paid by trekkers stays locally. Doug Scott sadly points out that the Sagarmatha National Park only has 2 per cent of its workforce drawn from the Sherpa community, while the rest are from the south of Nepal.

Doug Scott also points out that though we have plenty of declarations about what we must and must not do, they 'never mention the one thing every labourer in the trekking business really wants and that is a fair payment for his labours. The only sure way to improve the environment is to improve the wealth of the ordinary village in Nepal.' He feels that we should work round two main proposals: fix a minimum wage for porters as has been done in Pakistan; and determine a lower limit beyond which a trekking agency cannot quote.

In *Les Alpes*, August 1993, Trevor Braham pointed out that the 'millionaires' from the rich countries 'have invaded a country (Nepal) fundamentally poor and underdeveloped, in numbers which have attained frightening proportions—relative to what the fragile economy can support. These visitors demand, as much as possible, the commodities to which they are accustomed at home and for which they are prepared to pay. The prospect of quick riches which this represents for the local people is too good to forego, without regard to consequences such as the dislocation of their social and cultural heritage, the abandonment of their traditional occupations, the despoiling of their country, the exhaustion of their forest resources, the flood of garbage of western civilisation.' (Retranslated from the French, with apologies.)

Garbage and Waste

The rubbish at and above the Base Camp is awful, says Joss

Lynam, but doesn't do permanent damage; however the pollution of water supplies is serious. Among the easiest problems to solve, 'and probably the least important, are those connected with litter,' writes Mike Westmacott. 'On recent treks with reputable trekking agencies, I have been much encouraged by an apparent improvement in standards.' George Band was also pleasantly surprised to find things this year (1993) not as bad as he had expected. He has a genial idea for the much-publicised dump on South Col: pile up the empty oxygen cylinders into one great chorten in memory of those who did not return. Kurt Diemberger 'got the impression that a general consciousness regarding garbage is on its way, that mountaineers and trekkers widely use gas or other stoves (but much less is the case regarding their porter crew) and groups usually make toilet holes.'

'And above all, sensible packaging cuts down garbage', says Col. Sandhu. Robert McConnell also urges you to think before you leave and minimise the amount of packaging you bring. Buy local food, carry out toxic waste—batteries and medical waste—with you. The biggest problems are at the base camps and approaches. 'You are supported by local transport; you pay for the round trip and bring enough burlap or woven plastic bags for the garbage you will generate. And take care of what other thoughtless people have left behind.' Trevor Braham, in *Les Alpes*, January 1994, pointed out that Doug Scott and Serge Efimov, after attempting the Mazeno ridge to Nanga Parbat, burnt and buried 45 sacks of garbage collected in and around the Base Camp. In 1990, Mountain Wilderness organised a clean-up expedition to K2, as Kurt Diemberger reminds us.

He also urges Governmental decisions on 'where the garbage can be dumped or brought to for recycling.' While urging 'some kind of rubbish disposal system', Chris Bonington feels 'it is not realistic to expect trekkers to take their rubbish back with them, since as much is being generated by the local hotels and tea houses.' However, should we not remember that these exist only because there are trekkers?

Garbage may be only a cosmetic and minor defect, as Doug

Scott says, but he is quick to add that it is 'a symptom of a deeper malaise and lack of caring for wild and beautiful places.' And while Chris Bonington agrees that rubbish is primarily cosmetic, he points out that 'it does . . . demonstrate an attitude of mind and if trekkers, climbers and local people can be persuaded to dispose of their rubbish in a way that does not make a mess of the environment, it is a sound first step and base from which other more difficult and long-term actions can spring.' 'We can't actually solve any of the bigger problems until we solve this very simple one ourselves,' he had told the Tokyo Symposium.

Clean-up expeditions can never be a satisfactory answer. 'Parties going into the Khumbu to clean up other people's rubbish has to be a ridiculous system in the long-term,' Sir Edmund Hillary told the Tokyo Symposium. 'Mountaineers should be ashamed of leaving this rubbish,' said Buichi Oishi, President of the Green Earth Foundation on the same occasion.

Human Waste

Or shit, as Col. Dutt uncompromisingly calls it.

'The biggest problem today, I feel, is the lack of basic amenities i.e. disposal of human waste, . . .' wrote Col. Dutt. And Brig. Khullar pulls no punches in referring to the 'atrocious sense of public hygiene and sanitation of our people of the Indian subcontinent.'

'Human waste is probably the toughest issue . . . it is no longer possible to step romantically behind a bush,' writes Robert McConnell. 'Over the long-term solar or composting toilets should be purchased, installed and maintained on approaches and in base camp. We are going to have to pay for this. Near term, plan to bring along five-gallon plastic buckets with sealing lids for use as 'porta-potties' while on the approach and in base camps. The buckets fit neatly in a duffel bag and make great packing places (before use) for things you don't want to get wet or broken. One bucket per person is enough. On the way in, find farmers who want your manure for their fields. Often they will want the bucket even more.

As long as the buckets are sealed, for a bit of extra pay, porters, yak herders and others you rely on will carry it to where it can be used . . . The bucket approach will work and make base camps much pleasanter.

Perhaps the most encouraging experiment being carried out is the installation of solar toilets at the Base Camp, 4450 m of the Himalayan Mountaineering Institute (HMI), at Chaurikang. 'To start with, we made proper latrines,' writes Col. Dutt. 'I was also in a position to get the Solar Toilet Systems from USA and we installed it at our Base Camp. This toilet system works on a simple principle—the shit is cooked into ash before it becomes part of the soil . . . the Solar Toilet System is another relief as this can help in handling the amount of human shit all over the Himalayas. With the local materials, I have made a prototype model in Darjeeling so that the people can see it and feel inspired to handle all human wastes, which are day by day becoming a nuisance in the Himalaya.'

The story of this Solar Toilet System, told not only by Col. Dutt but by Joss Lynam, Robert McConnell and the Everest Environmental Project (EEP), Colorado Springs, USA, is particularly interesting. Michael Reynolds, an architect in Taos, New Mexico, was being successful with solar toilets and the EEP thought there might be something in this. When Robert McConnell met Col. Dutt, Principal of the HMI, at a Conference of the International Union of Alpinist Associations (UIAA) in Las Vegas in October 1992, they discussed possibilities of using these in the Himalaya. The HMI is host to 1400 students each year. Each student spends 10 days at Base Camp; 'at a pound a poop per day per student' as the EEP colourfully puts it, 'the HMI has to deal with approximately seven tons of human waste a year at Base Camp.'

Col. Dutt invited the EEP to install solar toilets at his Base Camp; Air-India transported them and gave the team reduced air fares; Indian Airlines donated transport from Delhi to Bagdogra. The Indian Mountaineering Foundation put the team up in Delhi; the HMI put them up in Darjeeling.

Ultimately, the team could take only one toilet with them. It left the US on 6 September 1993; in Delhi it discovered that the two boxes containing the parts of the solar toilet had not arrived. A blessing in disguise, because Michael Reynolds designed a 'fall back' option using local materials. The boxes eventually arrived but the Indian customs, true to their stereotyped image, wouldn't let them through, no doubt agonising over the seditious mysteries that a solar toilet might contain and wondering under what schedule customs duty should be computed.

The prototypes that Col. Dutt refers to were completed in less than a week the materials having been bought locally for about $100. They were taken to Base Camp where traditional toilets of open pits with burlap for screens were in use. The two solar toilets were installed in four days. Now one awaits a report on how they have worked. If successful, Michael Reynolds will write a manual on how to construct, install and maintain these toilets. A video of the work in Darjeeling and at Base Camp is available from the EEP for $15. 'If the toilets work as well as Michael anticipates, this technology will be useful in disposing of human waste not only at base camps but in villages and on trekking routes throughout the Himalaya,' says Col. Dutt.

By way of contrast, says Col. Dutt, a British medical team has announced its plans to install a solar toilet at the Everest Base Camp next spring. The British system will be constructed in England at an approximate cost of £10,000 ($20,000) and will then be shipped to Nepal. It would be interesting to have details of this and to learn to what extent it will meet the overwhelming needs of the Base Camp.

Aconcagua, the Everest of the Andes

An article in *Les Alpes*, August 1993, by Franco Giorgetta, draws a parallel between the crowds enticed by Aconcagua and by Everest. The 1991-92 season saw some 1200 persons on Aconcagua by mid-January. Halfway through the 1992-93 season, there had already been 1500.

A National Park was established two years ago and climbers have to register at Mendoza and pay $80 per person. Each one gets a numbered plastic garbage bag and the right to rescue services.

The bags have to be returned before leaving and are carried down to a depot on mules. From 1993, toxic and hard garbage is separated from the rest. The Sagarmatha National Park has a similar system. Expeditions must register at the park headquarters, Mendalphu, and deposit five Nepalese rupees for every kilo of equipment carried to base camps; these deposits are returned upon proper disposal of trash at Mendalphu or at the expense of the expedition.

There is a guardian at the base camp for Aconcagua but he finds it difficult to cope with the numbers. While some order is maintained there, the higher camps are filthy, with garbage and human waste everywhere. If each person stays an average of 10 days on the mountain, this means 15,000 'poops' of human waste. The German Alpine Club set an example by setting up a toilet tent. The author concludes that there is no alternative to self-discipline, sadly lacking.

Eco-Trekking

Col. Sandhu outlines the practical measures that he takes when trekking, measures within the possibility of everyone. Tony Streather provides us with the Alpine Club Policy Statement on climbing in the Alps and Greater Ranges, which is short and to the point. The International Union of Alpinist Associations (UIAA) has adopted a Himalayan Code of Conduct and this has also been issued by the Himalayan Environment Trust.

Particularly interesting is George Band's account of his 1991 Green Expedition to Bhutan. 'We aimed to observe an environmental code which we devised because the draft UIAA code was not finalised. Initially, we considered taking all bio-degradable refuse back to the capital Thimpu until we learnt that there was no disposal facility there! Instead, our aim was to dispose of all rubbish on trek by burning, crushing tins and giving away useful bottles and containers. In this way it was reduced to a very small quantity and then buried or carefully hidden under rocks. One difficulty was that burning refuse offended the more devout Buddhists in our party.'

'Regarding human waste, toilet tents were used in camp and the excreta buried. On the trail, it is a simple matter to burn the toilet paper and cover the excreta with earth, stones or leaves.' (Toilet paper—'the prayer flags of the tourists,' as someone called it.) Only dead wood was used for cooking.

Burying rubbish is better than leaving it lying around but it is not always 'a satisfactory solution,' as Chris Bonington points out. 'It gets uncovered either by animals or local people looking for items they can make use of.' The wind and birds also disperse rubbish.

The First Conference on National Parks and Protected Areas in East Asia, Beijing, 13-18 September 1993, stressed the need for effective management of protected areas and ecotourism.

Some Concluding Thoughts

What conclusions can we draw from all this? Nothing that hasn't been said dozens of times before but perhaps we can slant it a bit more towards possible action by individuals and their mountain clubs.

1. The fundamental problems of the Himalaya—overpopulation, poverty, overgrazing, deforestation, erosion, mass tourism outrunning the infrastructure, the infrastructure outrunning the carrying capacity of the region—are beyond our ken. Nevertheless we can, through our mountain clubs and other associations:

   a) ensure that the authorities of the eight Himalayan countries are under constant pressure to deal with these problems;
   b) promote ideas such as:

      — asking tourist agencies to collect voluntary contributions from their clients for afforestation projects;
      — 'twinning' a village with a climbing club so that the latter takes a special interest in the ecology of the area;
      — ensuring that some regions of the Himalaya, still untouched, remain inviolate or very severely protected;

— encouraging studies of the carrying capacity of different
regions so that numbers can be limited and not mind-
lessly increased;

— fixing minimum rates for porters and for agencies; and

— not being so dazzled by the larger problems that we
overlook the everyday, mundane ones of garbage, human waste and fuel which lie within our power to deal
with.

2. The United Nations system provides for input from recogni-
sed non-governmental organizations. We can, through our associations, influence the UN in its international and national programmes for the environment. Governments are sensitive to criticisms
voiced in international fora and we should take full advantage of
this.

3. We have no shortage of guidelines and codes. They stress
the need not to pollute, to burn and bury, to carry out hard and toxic
garbage, to use kerosene or gas, not to build 'toilets' near water
supplies, to respect local customs. Public opinion has been amply
sensitised. There have been Conferences, Seminars, Symposia,
Workshops, declarations, statements, resolutions. But should we
perhaps worry that while people are agitating in the capitals and
cities of the world, the local inhabitants are unaware of all this
furore and do not share it? Is there a gap between the awareness of
the distant environmentalist and that of the local peoples? We all
have a role to play in education and information. And do we visitors, fervent environmentalists at home, always live up to our own
code when visiting distant regions? Incidentally, how much time do
the various mountaineering institutes in India devote to environmental questions? One would hope that each person who completes
a course would be a dedicated environmentalist, setting a high standard himself and helping to enforce it.

4. Eco-tourism and Green expeditions: these must be the way
of the future. They are not really more difficult or more expensive
than the non-Green expedition. We could publicise practices re-
commended by Col. Balwant Sandhu and followed by expeditions
like those of George Band so that it will become a status symbol to

follow their footsteps: the greening of expeditions. We could report sub-standard tourist agencies—and sub-standard behaviour by expeditions—to our local journals; other journals could reproduce these reports so that the culprits are well and truly black-listed. Or if this is too strong medicine, then white-list the responsible agencies and expeditions. The *HJ* and the *Indian Mountaineer* of the Indian Mountaineering Foundation could set an example. Each *Alpine Journal* could have a regular section for such information on the Himalaya.

5. The busier camp sites are the main problems. There are often rubbish pits, but animals, wind and birds sometimes scatter what is deposited. Could not Liaison Officers organize the camps they happen to be in and enforce existing codes? Would it be possible to appoint full time local personnel in charge of campsites? Fees could be charged to finance these—say $2 per head per night—a small amount for the visitor, but generating enough funds to pay local employees. They should also be encouraged to sell specially marked garbage bags which the camper must arrange to have transported to the nearest depot. And may be honorary wardens could be appointed from among Liaison Officers, local personalities, members of Mountain Clubs and representatives of reputable agencies—analogous to Wild Life Wardens—with authority to ensure effective action?

6. There is no need to wait for Government action on this. Mountain clubs, individually or jointly, could appoint their own wardens who would have the authority of public opinion. (The Gangotri Conservation Project foresees a Chief Warden and three wardens). There could be a loosely constituted, open-ended Council of mountain clubs who would share experiences and information and publicise this, select a suitable insignia, and back up the actions of their wardens. Public opinion is sufficiently roused to support such voluntary action; indeed most visitors would welcome it. The UIAA or Mountain Wilderness could provide a framework for such a programme. Chris Bonington suggests an international conference run either by the UIAA or by the IUCN 'to come up with practical solutions that national mountaineering bodies and hopefully trekking companies could agree upon.' The Himalayan

Environment Trust already seems to be planning such a Conference in June 1994.

7. Human waste is a major problem at the more popular camp-sites. There is no doubt that there is a real and urgent need for permanent toilets and for ending the laissez-faire system that often prevails. If the Solar Toilet System works well at the HMI Base Camp, it would be a solution which could and should be general-ised. The permanent local personnel and honorary wardens men-tioned above could be responsible for the maintenance of these toilets. On the trail, each group should follow the Himalayan Code of Conduct and the example of the Green Expedition.

8. It is difficult to know to what extent kerosene, camping gas and garbage bags are available locally. Could not local entrepre-neurs be encouraged to sell these at strategic points? This would make the ban on the use of firewood easier to enforce. The same entrepreneur who sells garbage bags could collect them and ensure their transport to the nearest incinerator or depot, for a price.

9. We should anticipate problems before they overwhelm us. For instance, helicopter skiing and sightseeing have come to the Himalaya but not in a big way as yet. We could elaborate rules for this, marking out areas where this should be banned, before the situation gets out of hand. In Europe, while France has banned heliskiing, Switzerland still allows it and it is expanding despite energetic protests by environmental groups.

10. Ultimately, each visitor has to commit himself to a code of conduct and stick to it. Each individual visiting the Himalaya, every mountain club, has a responsibility for ensuring that this becomes a reality.

Thanks and Acknowledgements

I want to thank those who have contributed to this Symposium. All of them are very busy people and just the fact that they took the time and trouble to respond shows their concern for the Himalaya. It has been a privilege to have come into contact with so many outstanding mountaineers and I am grateful for the way in which they replied to my queries. It is the quality of their contributions that led to the decision to publish this Symposium in book form rather than as an article in the *HJ*.

Harish Kapadia, the editor of the *HJ*, is of course a phenomenon. The idea of this Symposium was first mooted in a chance conversation in Bombay (did not the Himalayan Club itself grow out of a 'chance conversation on Jakko Hill?') and was developed when Harish met members of the *Commission pour la protection de la nature alpine* of the Geneva Section of the Swiss Alpine Club, one of whom was about to set off for the Dhaulagiri region.

It was his personal friendship with leading 'Himalayanists' that elicited these contributions. He has provided advice and criticism and I am tempted to paraphrase one of P.G. Wodehouse's dedications: but for his constant help, this book would have been finished in half the time! And his comments came when he happened not to be in the Karakorams, or lecturing in the UK or Japan, or writing books on the Western Ghats, or attending meetings in Delhi, or editing the Journal. And oh yes, when he wasn't managing his business affairs.

My thanks to all.

The Green Expedition to Bhutan

GEORGE BAND

George Band is Chairman of the Alpine Club Library and a Trustee of the UK Branch of Sir Edmund Hillary's Himalayan Trust. He is a former President of the Alpine Club and Chairman of the Mount Everest Foundation. He was the youngest member of the 1953 Everest team; made the first ascent of Kangchenjunga with Joe Brown; has climbed in Peru and the Caucasus; in Bhutan in 1991; and revisited East Nepal in 1978 and 1993.

Major Environmental Problems of the Himalaya Today

— Deforestation of lower slopes for firewood and construction by inhabitants and or trekkers/climbers.
— Litter created by locals and trekkers/climbers.
— Overcrowding of the more popular peaks.

Dealing with Garbage, Toilets and Fuel

My recent experience has been on Everest Anniversary treks across East Nepal in 1978 and 1993, and to the Basingthang peaks in Bhutan in 1991. On the latter, initiated by Peter Mould and called the Green Expedition to Bhutan, we aimed to observe an environmental code which we devised and is appended because the draft UIAA (International Union of Alpinist Associations) Code was not finalised.

Initially, we considered taking all bio-degradable refuse back to the capital Thimpu until we learnt that there was no disposal facility there! Instead, our aim was to dispose of all rubbish on the trek by burning, crushing tins and giving away useful bottles and containers. In this way it was reduced to a very small quantity and then buried or carefully hidden under rocks. One difficulty was that burning refuse offended the more devout Buddhists in our party. In these circumstances, a larger volume had to be buried.

Regarding human waste, toilet tents were used in camp and the excreta buried. On the trail, it is a simple matter to burn the toilet paper and cover the excreta with earth, stones or leaves.

Only dead wood should be used for cooking fires, and trekkers should only indulge in camp fires in areas where dead wood is plentiful. I was glad to see this year (1993) that kerosene is being increasingly used in the Sagarmatha National Park and that indiscriminate tree felling is not allowed. In 1978 we were among the first trekkers required to pay a small fee to enter the park. If a smart trader had been set up at the entrance selling compulsory stoves and kerosene to trekking parties, he would be a millionaire by now!

Practical Measures to Deal with these Problems

Deforestation—No indiscriminate tree felling in National Park areas and encouragement to use kerosene or camping gas as much as possible for heating and cooking. The three tree nurseries set up in Khumbu by the Sir Edmund Hillary Foundation are an excellent initiative. The one we visited at Phurtse is producing some 30,000 three-year-old pine seedlings per year grown from seed for free distribution. About one million seedlings have been planted out since the Himalayan Trust began supporting this work, but it still only represents a drop in the ocean as survival is uncertain and the growth rate is very slow. Even so, this initiative should be extended throughout the Himalaya.

Litter—Although there has been considerable adverse publicity about the amount of litter along the trail to Everest, it was not as bad this year as I had been expecting. Many parts of Britain are in worse condition, particularly after a Bank Holiday weekend! The Sagarmatha Pollution Control Project is launching a public awareness and educational campaign to address this problem. Open rubbish pits are being provided at a number of regular camp sites but they are not altogether satisfactory; wind and birds can scatter the rubbish over a wide area. Burning is the best solution, provided local susceptibilities can be overcome.

The shameful photograph of debris and bodies on the South Col of Everest received wide publicity early this year. I appreciate that most climbers descending from the South Col feel lucky to be alive and have no energy left to tidy up before leaving. If an expedition is launched to help clear up this mess, I would suggest that the empty oxygen cylinders be piled up into one great chorten in memory of those who did not return.

Overcrowding—I support the substantial increase in peak fees imposed by the Nepalese Government from autumn this year for expeditions to Everest, particularly if a proportion of the revenue can be devoted to environmental protection. In the spring there were reports of some 19 expeditions to the mountain with several hundred climbers and Sherpas milling around the Base Camp. The increased fees should reduce the number of expeditions there to a more reasonable level and encourage smaller parties to visit less crowded areas.

Code of Conduct for Green Expedition to Bhutan

1. Be self-sufficient in fuel supplies except in areas of abundance of wood and then only use dead wood.
2. At camp sites, bury all bio-degradable rubbish and excreta. On the trail, cover it totally with earth, stones or leaves.
3. Carry out all non-bio-degradable items where practicable, otherwise completely bury under earth or stones.
4. Make sure that all washing and toilet activities do not pollute streams and water supplies.
5. Keep to paths where they exist.
6. Avoid damaging and removing plants.
7. Avoid disturbing and startling birds and animals.
8. When camping, replace turves and stones.
9. Respect religious shrines and artifacts.
10 Respect the customs and values of local people in conversation, dress and behaviour (includes not responding to begging for money or gifts).
11. For mountaineering expeditions, observe UIAA ethical code.

Alpine Club Policy Statement

TONY STREATHER

Lt. Col. H.R.A. Streather OBE was commissioned into
the Indian Army in 1945, posted to the NW Frontier and
remained there after Partition, with the Pakistan Army till
1950. It was that year that he reached the summit of
Tirich Mir with the Norwegians and this led to expeditions to Everest, K2 and Kangchenjunga and others.
He was President of the Alpine Club 1990-1992 and
has been President of the British Army Mountaineering
Association since 1976.

While I was President of the Alpine Club until the end of 1992,
we produced the following policy statement which may be of
some interest to you.

Climbing in the Alps and Greater Ranges

The Alpine Club is concerned about the protection of the environment, its people, its flora and fauna, and about the preservation
of the challenges which the mountains present to future generations.

In particular, the Club:

1. supports the use of protection and belaying techniques
   which cause minimal damage to the rock. Pegs, nuts, slings
   etc. which make use of natural rock features are felt to be
   acceptable but the use of bolts and the chipping or altering
   of rock features is deprecated.

2. believes that the mountains should be left as they are found. Equipment abandoned should be kept to an absolute minimum and no litter should be left on the approach, at base camp (or around huts), or on the mountain.

3. encourages small expeditions to the Greater Ranges which have minimal impact on the local environment.

Some Practical Measures at Base Camp

COL. AJIT K. DUTT

Col. Ajit Dutt, FRGS, SM, is Principal of the Himalayan Mountaineering Institute, Darjeeling. He has been climbing and trekking for over 20 years and has led or taken part in some 13 expeditions. He represented India at the UIAA Mountaineering Commission in 1991 and 1992. He is the author of several books, a booklet on *Mountain Manners*, and is the editor of the *Himalayan Mountaineering Journal*.

The Himalaya for the last two decades have been facing extreme pressure from the population explosion and a number of irresponsible tours organised for commercial purposes. The negative sign of damage can be felt and seen by anyone who has been visiting the Himalaya regularly, viz. vanishing forests, loss of rare animal species, serious changes in glacier shape, warming up of the total Himalayan environment. The issues are too many and one doesn't know, where the solution is. Poverty and the economic situation of the people living around the Himalaya adds to this environmental problem. New routes are opened, 20 expeditions reach the top of the Everest, 53 people climbed Everest in one day, but we have yet to see any infrastructure to accommodate abuses of such pressure on the Himalaya.

The biggest problem today, I feel, is the lack of basic amenities i.e., disposal of human waste, alternative sources of fuel for cooking, and safe drinking water. These are the worrying symptoms which need volunteer organisations and bureaucratic support. To start with it we made proper latrines at our Base Camp (4450 m) at

Chaurikhang in west Sikkim. Then we installed the Solar Toilet System. With local materials, I made a prototype model in Darjeeling and two such systems have been installed at our Base Camp—courtesy Bob McConnell of the American Alpine Club and his friend Michael Reynolds. This toilet system works on a simple principle: the shit is cooked into ash before it becomes part of the soil.

It is a great relief to us as this can help in handling the amount of human shit all over the Himalaya. However, its success at heights, say 15,000 ft. and beyond is not very encouraging, particularly in the eastern Himalaya where availability of the sun is low. I have yet to see its final products throughout the twelve months of the year. The experiment is on.

It has proved costlier, but we have been able to manage gas cylinders for all my HMI courses in the mountains thus totally dispensing with the requirement for wood. The concept of gas has been spread and for the last three years I have used the platform of HIMTAB (Himalayan Tourism Advisory Board) to impress upon all the tour operators to switch over to gas for cooking and help us in protecting our trees.

The Mountains, My Perspective

ROBERT M. McCONNELL

Robert McConnell is co-founder and Director of the
Everest Environmental Project; he led the 1990 and
1992 Everest Environmental Expeditions; in September
1993 he helped to install the Solar Toilet System at the
Base Camp of the Himalayan Mountaineering Institute.
He co-chairs the American Alpine Club Conservation
Committee, is the American delegate to the Interna-
tional Commission for Mountain Preservation, and is a
Fellow of the Explorers' Club.

We in the American Alpine Club, along with a growing number
of people in the mountaineering community internationally,
recognize the risk that adventure tourism in the Himalaya and spe-
cifically climbing expeditions in the Himalaya will, primarily as a
result of their increasing numbers, degrade the environment. Specific issues about which we are concerned include the inappropriate
disposal of human waste, unnecessary deforestation caused as expeditions travel on approaches into their base camps, and accumulation of garbage at base and higher camps. We are again, along
with many other groups, studying appropriate ways to deal with
these issues. We encourage travellers, including expeditions to the
Himalaya, to follow all regulations adopted by host countries. We
also provide each expedition a copy of *Trekking Gently in the
Himalaya* recently prepared by Wendy Brewer Lama in conjunc-
tion with the World Wide Fund for Nature. We also provide each
expedition a copy of the Kathmandu Declaration. Now that it has
been adopted by the UIAA General Assembly, we will also be
providing each expedition a copy of the UIAA Mountain Protection

Commission's 'Target Program Waste Disposal and Avoiding Trash.'

My personal views about the mountains are best summarized in the article recently published in *The American Alpine Club Journal*, 1993, which is reproduced below.

I have been asked to reflect about where we stand on protecting the mountains we love so much. The first thought that comes to mind is that we have turned an important corner in this effort. Alpinists today are increasingly aware of how fragile mountain environments are and how great an impact our adventures can have if we are not careful. The stories of trashed-out approaches and the photos of tents pitched on piles of garbage in base camps have caused many to reconsider the role they have played in creating these problems. The growing trend to close climbing areas in many countries and to close entire mountain ranges in others has brought home the need to address the problem now.

Today we face another challenge. Awareness is not enough. Awareness must be translated into action. We must each adopt a personal commitment to leave as little trace as possible of our passing through the mountains. That personal commitment should be part of our planning for every trip. A plan to deal with packaging, food scraps and human waste as it is generated at each stage of the trip from approach to return is essential. In order for the plan to work, it should be shared with and agreed to by the entire team and its support staff before departure.

Human waste is probably the toughest issue to address and so I'll start with it. There are those among us who seem to romanticize stepping behind a bush or digging a cat hole when they squat to contemplate the meaning of life. Anything else seems to get in the way of their enjoyment of the great outdoors to hear them tell it. Well, they are living in a fantasy world, as least as far as popular climbs are concerned. The fact is that in too many places, there aren't any more bushes to step behind without stepping in someone else's previous deposit. All too often there isn't anywhere to dig without digging into what someone else left behind.

So what is the answer? Over the long term, solar or composting toilets should be purchased, installed and maintained on approaches and in base camps. We who use these areas are going to have to pay for this. Near term, plan to bring along five-gallon plastic buckets with sealing lids for use as "porta-potties" while on the approach and in base camps. The buckets fit neatly in a duffel bag and make great packing places (before use) for things you don't want to get wet or broken. One bucket per person is enough. On the way in, find farmers who want your manure for their fields. Often they will want the bucket even more. As long as the buckets are sealed, for a bit of extra pay, porters, yak herders and others you rely on will carry it to where it can be used. Not as romantic as a bush, but then, there are other ways to work out romantic fantasies. Try it. The bucket approach will work and make base camps much pleasanter.

By thinking before you leave, you can minimize the amount of packaging you bring. You can rely as far as possible on buying food in local centres when you travel in developing countries. This eliminates even more packaging and stimulates the local economy. One way to do this is to send your support staff a shopping list. Have them confirm what they have bought before you leave so you can fill in around the edges. This thought process is critical because most packaging becomes garbage during a trip.

In nearly all mountainous areas, wood is a precious commodity. Climbing expeditions and trekking groups should *never* burn wood, which takes years to regenerate and in many places rarely grows back. This also causes devastating erosion. Campfires, for all their romantic appeal, are *taboo*. Wood must not be used for cooking. It is easy enough to insist that visitors to the mountain use portable cooking stoves to prepare their food. It is more difficult to enforce this prohibition of cooking and heating fires on the porters. They must be given stoves and instructions for their use. Fuel has to be rationed to them so that they don't burn it all up in a short time. This prohibition can be enforced if there is a clear understanding with the Sirdar that absolutely no wood may be burned.

Another issue that needs advance planning is "toxic" waste. I use the term to mean anything that cannot be safely disposed of in remote areas. Again, minimizing the amount you bring is an important first step. Solar rechargers can reduce the number of batteries you need for extended trips. The batteries you do use and any medical waste you generate should be brought out of the mountains. Your plan should include how you will pack out with you anything that won't burn or decompose.

When planning is finally done and the trip is underway, the personal commitment to leaving as little trace as possible of your passing should be part of your thought process every day. The higher you go, the tougher this becomes. But no one can justify leaving a mess behind with the argument that a climb is too far out on the edge to do it right. Doing it right means doing it in such a way as to leave no trace of your passing.

Fortunately, the greater number of people and therefore the biggest problems are at the base camps and on the approaches. Anywhere you are supported by local transportation, whether it is porters, yaks, camels or trucks, the answer is easy. You pay for the round trip use of the transportation, you bring enough burlap or woven plastic bags for all the garbage you will generate and you bring out whatever won't burn or decompose. And take care of what other thoughtless people have left. Anything less is no longer acceptable. Those who object to the extra cost, to supervising those you hire and the time it takes should look to other sources of personal challenge, spiritual growth and enjoyment rather than climbing.

The last issue I want to address is what happens when someone else screws up. Some of what I have said will be unacceptable to some climbers. I welcome their thoughts and the opportunity to debate these issues. However, all of us realize a base level of unacceptable behaviour. You may not be able to define it, but you know it when you see it.

Himalayan Environment

JOSS LYNAM

Joss Lynam was born in 1924 and has been climbing and walking all his life. He has taken part in nine Himalayan expeditions, mostly as leader, ranging from Kashmir in 1946 to Garhwal in 1991; he has made climbing trips to Greenland, the Andes, the Rockies and East Africa; and he has walked and climbed extensively in Ireland, Britain and the Alps. He is Chairman of the Expeditions Commission of the International Union of Alpinist Associations (UIAA), Chairman of the National Long Distance Walking Routes Committee of Ireland, Executive Member of the Mountaineering Council of Ireland (MCI). He edits the *Irish Mountain Log*, the official publication of the MCI and has edited a number of walking guide books to Ireland.

The damage to the Himalayan environment can be divided into five categories, which I am listing in what I consider is their ascending order of importance:

1. Rubbish and pollution above the Base Camp—fixed ropes, oxygen bottles, faeces, general detritus.
2. Rubbish at and below the Base Camp level—tins, plastic, faeces.
3. Pollution of water supplies.
4. Sociological damage.
5. Deforestation.

As a climber I detest the rubbish that I find on the mountain, it enormously reduces my enjoyment. But, to be objective it does not do any permanent damage either to the mountain or to any human, and is it very expensive (and dangerous) to remove. To be cynical, no one is going to stop climbing Everest just because of the rubbish on the South Col. Complain, yes; stop climbing, no.

Climbers and trekkers are revolted by the rubbish and pollution which exists at the Base Camps and below in any popular climbing and trekking area. Again, it does not do permanent damage to the environment; in the long run it may damage the local economy if trekkers go elsewhere. On the other hand, this class of rubbish is relatively easy and cheap to remove.

Pollution of water supplies is a very serious matter. It is a function of heavy usage and human excreta is a major cause.

Sociological damage—The economies of the Khumbu and Skardu-Askole area have been revolutionised in the last few decades. Agricultural economies have been turned into tourist service economies. Subsistence farming has been replaced by commercialism. Climbers and trekkers (particularly trekkers) are eating the local produce—food has to be imported. There's more money around but it is unevenly distributed and it is reckoned that in one of the best organised trekking areas (Annapurna) only about 10 per cent of the money paid by trekkers stays locally. *Over-rapid development has caused more harm than good. "Sustainable Development" is the cliché of the decade, but that doesn't make it any less true.

Deforestation—For me this is the worst feature of the modern changes in the Himalaya. No need to restate the dire effects of deforestation, we all know them, and we know that without enormous resources they are irreversible. Because the effects are almost irreversible, for me deforestation must be a main target of our work to protect the Himalaya. Of course it isn't just mountaineers and trekkers; a whole host of other groups are busy cutting trees—pilgrims, land-hungry farmers and commercial loggers are at least as responsible. But it would help if *we* behave ourselves.

What should we as mountaineers be doing to improve the Himalayan (and every other mountain) environment? We can divide action into curative and preventive.

Curative action—Without wishing to denigrate the unselfish hard work put in by cleaning expeditions, I don't think that they are the answer, except in so far as they highlight the problem. Much more to the point is that every expedition should not only ". . . leave nothing but footprints" (and not too many of them please!) but should take out more than they bring in. This is particularly true of rubbish above the Base Camp. No one should be risking his life to bring out someone else's rubbish.

Preventive action—I pass over the obvious steps which climbers should take to reduce rubbish, to remove what they do bring with them, and to eschew wood fires both for themselves and their porters—these are very well covered in the handouts from UIAA, DAV Summit Club, Himalayan Environment Trust etc. I think every visitor who is *prepared to listen* has got the message. What needs to be highlighted now are the other steps that are necessary to slow deforestation and improve the rubbish and pollution rubbish disposal.

Education—Local people must be educated; more than one expedition has seen its carefully-collected rubbish deposited along the return trail by porters anxious to reduce their loads. This is a pity; local people who have to live with deforestation and with the other impacts of trekkers and climbers on their land could be the best possible environmental policemen. Nor is education just for locals. For all the lip-service governments pay to environmental protection, when the chips are down they almost invariably plan for short-term gain. As long as Market Forces are God, it is going to be almost impossible to protect the Himalaya.

Excuse the rhetoric, we won't change the way world thinks with one symposium—let me get to some practicalities. Information—I would like to see every tourist and pilgrim group handed a sheet telling them what to do about environmental protection *in the area they are visiting*. I don't mean general remarks like "don't use firewood" and "bring tins back to roadhead", I mean an actual statement of where kerosene can be bought and where the tin crusher is located. Vague exhortations simply disenchant climbers and trekkers who are already too prone to criticise host countries for corruption and bureaucracy. ("What is happening to the money we pay as an environmental levy?")

Facilities and materials—The host countries have so many other problems that the developed countries must help with ideas and technology as well as money. Bob McConnell by developing and donating solar toilets is showing the way. There are such actions I know, but not nearly enough, and while I applaud these actions, I fear they are only nibbling at the problem.

We urgently need an integrated policy dealing with practicalities in terms which people can readily translate into action. This isn't something which will be done by a Conference or Seminar. An environmentalist (or a team?) must look at a pilot area, consult with all those involved, both official and unofficial, users and locals, and finally produce a detailed pragmatic plan:

* Fuel—how much and where.
* Rubbish—how and where to dispose of paper, plastic, metals, etc.
* Usage of local food and materials—what is permissible, what is not.
* Developments which will help the environment.

In sum, a tourist blueprint for the pilot area.

If such a blueprint existed, it would be relatively simple to work out how to apply it to other areas.

The Himalayan Environment Trust or some similar body should be asked to fund the study.

Before it is Too Late

MICHAEL WESTMACOTT

Michael Westmacott is President of the Alpine Club and was Chairman of the Alpine Club Library 1985-92 when he set up the Himalayan Index covering 2000 peaks, 4000 expeditions and 3000 literary references. Has climbed extensively in the Andes and Alaska as well as in the Himalaya, with several first ascents including Huagaruricho (Peru).

The Hon. Editor has sent down a fast one—or is it a googly? I was never a cricketer. How is it possible now to say anything new or interesting about protection of the mountain environment? Yet how is it possible *not* to contribute to the Symposium? One would be accused of ignoring the problem as well as the Hon. Editor.

The problems are various, but all stem from the ever-increasing number of local residents, trekkers and climbers in the Himalaya, and the rising material standards demanded by all of them. Most of us, when we enjoy hot washing water, do not think of the time a tree takes to grow. Most of us do not want to carry away useless damaged equipment or empty tin cans. The first step in any effort at conservation is to make people aware. In the West, a lot is spoken and written about protection of the environment; no one has any excuse for ignorance, though we must be reminded again and again if we are to remember. I am not competent to say whether, in the Himalayan countries themselves, enough is said and done to ensure that their people, particularly those who live and work in the hills, are aware of the long-term damage all of us can do if we are not careful—but I doubt it.

Being more specific, the easiest problems to solve, and probably the least important, are those connected with litter. On recent treks with reputable trekking agencies, I have been much encouraged by an apparent improvement in standards. The trails of Nepal and the alleys of Namche Bazar are cleaner than the streets of my London suburb and cleaner of course than Kathmandu. A combination of peer pressure and host government pressure should ensure that a majority of the agencies converge towards the high standards of the best of them. Individual back-packers are impossible to control, but will respond to peer pressure and well-aimed publicity. Over-used campsites do need some regulation. I recently saw a photo of a mess tent full of Liaison Officers, one for each of 6 or 8 expeditions to an 8000er. Surely it is not too much to ask of this concentration of talent that they should organise a campsite in order to minimize its impact. L.O.'s also have to ensure that expeditions do not economise too much on porterage for the return journey, and that all 'hard' litter is carried out.

Far more important is the degradation of the lower slopes due to wood cutting for building and for fuel, the latter mainly for the use of locals and porters but also for facilities for tourists. Here the key must ultimately be in the hands of the local communities, more of which should be encouraged, or even compelled, to set limits to wood cutting, in their own long-term interest. Easy to say, but very hard to implement. It cannot be done just by legislative fiat; only be persistent education. And control over the gathering of fuel must be accompanied by availability of kerosene or other alternatives.

What is the Alpine Club doing about all this? We do not as a Club organise or sponsor expeditions, but we encourage our members and, through the Mount Everest Foundation, likewise encourage other British expeditions to respect the environment and the interests and wishes of local people. The effects of increasing numbers are painfully obvious to those of us who have been climbing for 40 years or more. What we must all do is to educate those now going to the hills before it is too late.

Himalaya: Our Fragile Heritage

N.D. JAYAL

N.D. Jayal is Director-General (Natural Heritage) of the Indian National Trust for Art and Cultural Heritage (INTACH), with the responsibility of promoting the conservation of our natural heritage. His expeditions to the Himalaya include Trisul (1951), Kamet (1952), Nun-Kun (1953) and Lahul Triangle (1954).

As a senior civil servant in the Ministry of Environment, he was instrumental in the declaration of the Nanda Devi Sanctuary and its surroundings as a National Park/Biosphere Reserve and subsequently a World Heritage Site. He played a key role in the establishment of National Parks/Biosphere Reserves in Ladakh, Himachal Pradesh, Garhwal Himalaya, Sikkim and Arunachal Pradesh.

He has sent us his brochure entitled *Himalaya: Our Fragile Heritage*; after an introductory paragraph, some extracts are published below.

There is a tendency to look upon the environmental problems of the mountains as largely relating to the accumulation of garbage left by trekkers and mountaineers. Littering the mountains is of course reprehensible and everything possible should be done to keep our mountains free of such pollution.

However, a much more serious environmental problem in the fragile Himalaya concerns their limited carrying capacity in terms of the natural, productive, life-supporting endowments of vegetation, soil and water. Excessive destructive development and human intrusion, whether of indigenous rising populations and settlers, or visitors in the form of tourists, trekkers or mountaineers, beyond their carrying capacity, is already causing serious concern with often irreversible ecological degradation of large areas. To correct these human aberrations for saving the Himalaya, a broader, socially and ecologically sound, conservation and sustainable development strategy is, more than ever before, an imperative necessity.—Ed.

With the extension of communications and increasing urbanisation, the influx of large numbers of people from outside, into the farthest reaches of the Himalaya can easily imperil its sensitive ecosystems. Unadapted to outside processes, the communities and cultures within such ecosystems could lose their identity and quality, or perish altogether. Opening up of mountains facilitates exploitation of resources, hydro power, minerals, timber, plants and animal produce to such an extent that greed overtakes and undermines not only the mountains but also the vast plains below. This is the plight of the Himalaya today and, with it, the very foundation of human societies in the Gangetic and Brahmaputra valleys are endangered.

There were always a few people in the hills who subsisted on minimum resources from large areas. However, with 'development,' waves of people with a new philosophy of life based on the market economy entered the mountains and introduced an exploitative approach which has disrupted the erstwhile delicate balance. Forests were taken away from community ownership and reserved for meeting commercial requirements of timber in the plains. A network of roads was extended into the mountains for exploitation of timber, plant and mineral resources. And gigantic hydro-power schemes to support industries elsewhere were launched. At the same time, the human and domestic animal populations of hill communities also increased, adding to the already heavy pressures on the limited natural resources of the mountains.

With the disappearance of vegetation on an extensive scale, water and fuel resources dwindled and soil rapidly lost its productivity. This has led not only to large scale migration of the hill people to the plains for their survival, but also made it impossible for those left behind to survive without great hardship in their desperate search over long distances for fuel and water.

This indeed was the genesis of the now famous 'Chipko' movement in the hills, with the realisation by the remnant hill communities, comprising largely womenfolk, that their survival depended upon the protection of their life-supporting water and soil resources provided by the forests.

The change in land-use patterns brought about by substituting mixed natural forests by monoculture pine plantations led to accelerated soil erosion. This, coupled with a rapid increase in population, forced a majority of able-bodied men to seek employment in cities in the plains. The main burden of managing the family and caring for the aged, the children and cattle, and carrying on agricultural operations, thus fell on the shoulders of the womenfolk. They walk long distances to collect such basic necessities of life as water, fuel and fodder, rendered scarce by the loss of tree cover. Under the inspiration of various disciples of Gandhiji and Sarvodaya workers, the process of educating the masses through folk songs, footmarches, and so on began, and the following slogan was popularised: "What do the forests bear? Soil, water and pure air. Soil, water and pure air are the basis of life."

Another dimension to the pressures of development activities mentioned above was introduced by tourism and mountaineering, rapidly gaining popularity during the short summer months. Foreigners were allowed access to many hitherto prohibited areas, and streams of expeditions to a number of popular peaks led to serious depletion of the limited biological wealth during the crucial growth period in the few summer months. The ingress of scores of large expeditions each year into the Nanda Devi Sanctuary is a classic example of rapid resource depletion of a unique marvel of nature's mountain architecture, where scores of endemic species have evolved under natural protection for a millenia. The slow growth of the plants can be judged from the fact that at high altitudes the birch tree attains a diameter of two centimetres in six years while a juniper bush takes twenty years for the same growth. To save such priceless heritage areas from destruction, it became inevitable to extend them protection in order to facilitate the slow process of restoration of their biological and natural assets. In these circumstances, national natural heritage areas such as Nanda Devi Sanctuary and the Valley of Flowers have been accorded total protection from all forms of human interference, except for purely scientific work, and have been set aside as national parks or biosphere reserves.

Mountains must be our refuge for contemplation and recreation, and for many societies their very survival depends on them. But before irretrievable damage is done, we must carefully assess to what limits the system can be exploited or developed. We have seen that even non-consumptive exploitation such as tourism or mountaineering can cause havoc, unless planned with meticulous care and consideration for the fragility of the ecosystem. The Himalaya are also a sensitive international border, subject to development of people requiring a network of strategic roads which should not be constructed thoughtlessly and destructively. The ecological hazards of constructing major dams in the Himalaya and their environmental implications should be fully realised. It is clear that a massive rehabilitation programme is urgently needed to save the Himalaya from serious ecological degradation. A comprehensive resource survey, and planned integrated development with river catchment areas as units, keeping long range perspectives in view, are the key elements for restoring the complex Himalayan ecosystems.

The Himalaya, the world's youngest and highest mountains, are unique in many other aspects. This mountain range, arranged in three distinct folds, links up three very diverse biological regions of the world—the very rich Malayan tropical bio-geographic region, the cold temperate Eurasia and the monsoon Indian peninsula. There is, in fact, a very attenuated connection even with the African-Arabian region. Plants and animals have found a haven in very valuable niches of the Himalaya, which now need to be identified and protected as biosphere reserves—an international network of protected areas with representative examples of landscapes, each with its characteristic floral, faunal and human uses—where evolution of life can continue in its totality in natural habitats. Areas capable of exploitation for various uses need to be identified and the carrying capacity of each area assessed within a comprehensive management plan. Mass influx of visitors to popular areas will need to be controlled by reducing access and amenities to conform to carrying capacities. Detailed land evaluation surveys and land capability classification are, therefore, an essential prerequisite for avoiding the kind of mistakes which can only be corrected subsequently at great cost.

Any programme for managing and developing our mountain areas should always consider the delicate cultural balance the hill people have evolved to survive in their often very harsh environment. It is easy to destroy this balance by the large scale advent of modern cultures and values which are often brazenly exploitative. The denudation of the Central Himalaya has already created disturbing sociological problems leading to emigration and to eco-disasters in adjacent areas. For the hill peoples, very carefully drawn up plans of direct relevance to them need to be implemented, to buffer them against cultural shocks and ease the pressure on their largely subsistence-level existence. Schumacher's concept of "small is beautiful" epitomises the approach to the development of our fragile mountains and their sequestered inhabitants which must carefully set aside projects of great eco-destructive potential.

Environmental Protection: A Complex Question

CHRIS BONINGTON

Chris Bonington, CBE, is perhaps the best known name in mountaineering today. He has opened many new routes in Britain and the Alps; he has led and been on 17 Himalayan expeditions, including 4 to Everest which he climbed in 1985 at the age of 50; he has several first ascents in different parts of the world to his credit; he led the successful Annapurna South Face Expedition, 1970, the first ascent of a Himalayan big wall, and the successful Everest SW Face Expedition, 1975. He has written 13 outstanding books and presented and appeared in many TV programmes, including a re-play of Mummery's first ascent of the Grépon. He now seems to delight in small expeditions to lesser known areas.

The question of environmental protection is a complex one, the solution to which needs to be looked at on different levels.

Rubbish

This is the most obvious, the easiest to deal with and yet in some ways the least important of environmental problems, for it is primarily cosmetic. It does however demonstrate an attitude of mind and if trekkers, climbers and local people can be persuaded to dispose of their rubbish in a way that does not make a mess of the environment, it is a sound first step and base from which other more difficult and long-term actions can spring.

Effective steps are already being taken in some of the most popular areas. In Solo Khumbu the Sherpas have formed the

'Sagarmatha Pollution Control Project' which, with the help of a grant from the World Wide Fund for Nature, has dug approximately eighty refuse holes and has arranged a collection from these to a central dump. This kind of local action seems by far the most effective. It is also important in any area where trekking and tourism has become an important part of the local economy that some kind of rubbish disposal system is instituted. It is not realistic to expect trekkers to take their rubbish back with them, since as much is being generated by the local hotels and tea houses.

In areas which have not become part of the tourist trail, it probably is best if trekkers and expeditioners do take everything back with them, since burying rubbish is not a satisfactory solution. It gets uncovered either by animals or local people looking for items they can make use of.

Expeditions also need to start planning ways of removing their rubbish from the mountain. Some of the more popular climbs on 8000 m peaks in particular, are an appalling mess because there has been no effort to take rubbish back down. The pressure on Himalayan peaks means that unless climbers raise this issue to a priority as high as getting to the summit itself, the mountains of the Himalaya are going to become a giant rubbish tip. Dropping rubbish into crevasses is not a solution, since sooner or later it will be disgorged. It is much better to plan on taking everything down and keep packaging to a minimum in consequence.

Deforestation

This is a much wider issue than that of rubbish since the impact of tourism is only part of the cause. This can be addressed by trekking and climbing groups using their own stoves and refraining from lighting fires. In this respect however they also need to provide stoves for porters. The question of local houses, tea houses and hotels is a more difficult problem since wood is still the main fuel. Improved stoves combining back boilers cut down fuel consumption but do not remove it. Wider use of hydro-electric power seems the best solution but this entails both investment and the provision of effective maintenance.

In addition there is the question of clearing timber to provide more agricultural land as populations rise and more building materials not only locally but also for the towns are required. This latter is a particular problem in Tibet where they are rapidly destroying their forests. These problems need decisions to be taken at the governmental level, but the mountaineering community should add its voice to the need for action.

An effective international conference would undoubtedly be useful. Since the question of rubbish and also the use of fuel by trekkers and climbers is something that can be directly solved, I recommend a conference run either by the UIAA or by IUCN (International Union for the Conservation of Nature) to come up with practical solutions that national mountaineering bodies and hopefully trekking companies could agree upon.

Himalayan Tourism and the Market Economy

DOUG SCOTT

Doug Scott has been mountaineering in the Himalaya since 1966; he has been on some 35 expeditions on various continents and has spent a total of 3 years in Nepal and a year in India. His climbs have included the SW face of Everest with Dougal Haston in 1975; Changabang in 1974; the Ogre with Chris Bonington in 1977 when he broke both legs in a fall and had an epic descent; Kangchenjunga in 1979; the North face of Nuptse the same year; and Shisha Pangma in 1982. In 1990 he helped to start the Specialist Trekking Cooperative now being organized by Sharu Prabhu and Ang Phurba. He wrote this article for *Himal Magazine*, Kathmandu; some extracts are published below.

Thirty years ago, the first of those to have fallen under the spell of the Himalaya stayed behind to organise journeys for others, so as to be there more permanently and to make a living from providing such a service. That was Jimmy Roberts, followed a few years later by Mike Cheney, who both set the standards which have been observed by the better trekking companies ever since.

Now there are more than two hundred trekking agencies in Kathmandu alone, and the number is growing all the time, there and elsewhere throughout the Himalaya and Karakoram mountains. The Government of Nepal is planning to increase the number of tourists to its country from the present 300,000 to 1,000,000 by the end of the century. Tourism already accounts for a quarter of that country's foreign earnings, of which trekking is a large part. In the West new agencies continue to set up and vie with each other in advertising the Himalayan-bound clients. It is now big business with few constraints. There are no bounds to the growth of this industry, particularly in the Third World as industrialism and transportation improve and remain relatively inexpensive.

Tourism has now overtaken petroleum as the world's largest industry, but it is just as exhaustive of its own resource, as is petroleum. For it has been said that tourism destroys tourism, especially in the case of mountain tourism. Most visitors choose to go to the mountains for peace and quiet, and escape from hectic city life to another reality.

The alarm bells are ringing throughout the European Alps and 'Alp Action' is swinging into gear to curb the gross commercialisation, the overcrowding which has led to pollution from exhaust fumes, acid rain and decaying forests, and all the slopes which are strung with ski tows and lifts.

Those who still require the serenity of the hills, they can always go to the Himalaya. Ah! but that is not to say that there aren't problems there. For, as everyone knows, Everest is now a rubbish tip, and trekkers and climbers have helped cause deforestation, land slides and flooding. Sweep away the rubbish, use kerosene, and the problem is solved—or so everyone thinks. Actually the rubbish and discarded equipment left on the mountain side is not of world-shattering importance. It is only a cosmetic and minor defect, albeit a symptom of a deeper malaise and lack of caring for wild and beautiful places. It is debatable as to how much the tourist has caused the deforestation on Himalayan hillsides. It is, in fact, negligible when compared with the demands of the ever burgeoning population.

The number of climbers, trekkers and mountain tourists increase. Is this increase sustainable from the point of view of the indigenous population and the visitor? The visitors once trickled quietly into Nepal; how do they respond now the floodgates are open—now they come en masse—now there is mass tourism?

Himalayan Climbing

Overcrowding on the popular 8000 m peaks does not worry

everyone but mainly those who knew the Himalaya when there were restrictions on access, who were used to having the mountain to themselves and those newcomers who are more discerning. The majority seem content just to be there, albeit with as many as fifty other people, all plodding up the same route as themselves, as witnessed by the author in 1988 on the original route of Makalu. Nowadays, there can be more than one hundred people strung out on the ordinary route of Everest. Many of these people will not be mountaineers in the true sense of the word, for they have hired others to make decisions for them, to pass judgement as to whether it is right to continue or to retreat, to pick out a route, to select a safe campsite, and more often than not to carry most of the load and complete the majority of the camp chores. This is the modern breed of high mountain tourist who has bought his way onto that mountain rather than having earned his place by dint of serving a long apprenticeship.

This facet of tourism is set to expand rapidly as it is now known just how big the financial gain is. More and more climbers will drop out of climbing for themselves in order to capitalise on the need of others to be guided—so far, only up what the Sherpas call 'the Yak route' of Everest. This is only an extension of guiding in the Alps, which has a long and honourable tradition, but, of course, Everest is not in a sophisticated European country—it is in Nepal, a third-world country, without the infrastructure to cope with the influx of visitors—more about this later. Also, it is a lot higher than Mont Blanc, and potentially more dangerous. Climbers will be lured into a false sense of security by the large number of other people around although, when the storm comes, it's every group for itself, if not every man for himself. Still it is obvious that it is less of an adventure when so many other people are on the same mountain. The golden age is always in the past, unfortunately. We were so lucky, those of us who were climbing ten years ago to have had the joyful experience of a whole mountain to ourselves. Regular non-commercial amateur climbers have expressed resentment at being there with so many others. They would prefer a return to the days of restriction and are prepared to wait their turn if it means peace and quiet.

Trekking

The same observations must apply to those trekking along Himalayan valleys, who will obviously much prefer not to have the distraction of so many other trekking groups on their heels or to be sharing campsites like that in front of the Tengboche Monastery with anything up to 150 other people. They will resent going off into the surrounding woodland to find so many others had already relieved themselves there too. Leave no stone unturned and no . . . Mainly it is the distraction from entering into the spirit of the mountains and appreciating the local people that mass trekking causes.

The Land

There is no doubt that tourism has brought great material benefit to many Nepalese and hill farmers and pastoralists throughout the high mountains of Asia. However, the Nepalese Government has encouraged tourism without taking much account of its effect on the physical environment. It is time the carrying capacity of each area was worked out in a thoroughly scientific manner. For instance, did anyone at Head Office, on lifting restrictions, stop to consider where the 500-1000 people who may be at Everest Base Camp at any one time could evacuate their human waste, there, and on the walk up? Most schemes which have improved the situation have by-passed the Central Government, as it is either too bureaucratic, inefficient and/or corrupt.

It has been the Sherpas themselves who have cleaned up Sagarmatha, with the financial help of the World Wide Fund for Nature. With that help, the Sherpa people were able to pay and organise themselves to dig some eighty pits for the disposal of rubbish. This is still an ongoing problem, as what to do with that rubbish has yet to be decided. Self-help schemes are definitely the way forward. Outside charity hand-outs can have a weakening effect on local society. In the case of the Sherpas helping collect rubbish they will now be more aware of the problem themselves. We all have to be educated to see a tin can or a plastic wrapper as no longer just that but also as litter. It was the World Wide Fund for Nature that supported the Annapurna Conservation Area Project. It has done such a fantastic job in the Annapurna region, especially with controlling destruction of the forests. The New Zealanders have planted huge areas of Khumbu with conifers for the distant future as, at that altitude, they only grow a few inches per year. It is a good thing for the Sherpa people to see how long it takes for a tree to grow and what a valuable commodity a tree is. Sadly, the Sagarmatha National Park only has 2 per cent of its workforce drawn from the Sherpa community, the rest are from the south of Nepal. Similarly, the fees paid on the gate leading into the Sagarmatha National Park do not go directly to the benefit of the Sherpa people, but to the central exchequer for distribution all over Nepal. Whilst this may be good in theory, in practice of course, much of that money will be lost in administrative costs and sheer corruption. One wonders why fifty soldiers are needed to patrol the park and what impact they have on limited resources?

So the visitor is now aware that he mustn't pollute, he must burn, bash and bury, or remove his garbage, and he must not burn wood, nor must his staff. Everyone must cook and heat on kerosene. The Himalayan Tourist Code is on everyone's lips and has done much to improve the environment. There are declarations made every year at prestigious conferences about this, but they never mention the one thing every labourer in the trekking business really wants and that is a fair payment for his labours. So there is still pressure on the land all over Nepal and the rest of the Himalaya because of increase in population and of the growing poverty of the poorer strata of society.

The only sure way to improve the environment is to improve the wealth of the ordinary villager of Nepal. For only then will he be able to afford fossil fuel, energy-efficient stoves, and only with a better income from elsewhere will he cease slashing and burning the marginal land and stop pushing his animals up to the limit of vegetation and growing things. Thus it would be of great benefit to the environment and to conservation, if money from tourism were to find its way down to the lowly porter. This, at the moment, hardly happens. Of the money the client pays his trekking agent, only 10 per cent, at the very most, will be the wages of the Sirdar, cookboys, Naike, and the porters. Usually the percentage is a lot lower than that. Unlike Pakistan, trekking tourism in Nepal is almost completely without regulation. It is market economy in the raw, starting with the Western agent shopping round for the lowest reasonable quote, from the 200 + agents in Kathmandu, who are so desperate for business they will promise the earth, and try to deliver, and may be they will to the Western agent, but not to their own. The Sirdar will be given so little to pay his staff and then what is left goes to the Naike and the porters. Corruption is rife in Nepal—it comes from above; just as Prime Minister Thatcher put her stamp on British political and social life, so the King and his Ministers have for thirty years ruled the country by patronage so that 250,000 civil servants were beholden to the monarchy.

The Sherpas are not immune to ripping off the less fortunate and it is very difficult to make an arrangement whereby the Sherpa Sirdar will pay the full amount allowed to the porters without him and the Naike colluding to cream off a percentage. One way around the whole problem is to work to implement two main proposals:

a) *Minimum Wage for the Porters*

To fix a minimum wage for the porters in excess of the lowly wretched wage currently offered. It varies from place to place, but may well be as little as 60 rupees per day (80p) in the Annapurna region; it is, of course, all a matter of supply and demand. Why should there be room for manoeuvre here in saving money? If trekkers/mountaineers can't afford to pay, they shouldn't be going to the Himalaya until they have raised sufficient finance. It is a pathetic excuse to suggest the porters will only spend extra money on alcohol or drugs, or that by paying a basic wage of say £2 per day it will lead to inflation. This is the sort of argument put by local agents in the big urban areas. They are responsible, along with the Sirdars, for not paying adequate and fair wages to the porters. Incidentally, there are minimum wages set by the Ministry of Tourism in Nepal for local porters working for mountaineering expeditions. It is currently in force at 26 rupees—about 30p. per day!

There are many regulations, both National and European, that are designed to safeguard the tourist travelling abroad and to third-world countries, but there's not one regulation that I have seen, not even a suggestion, as to how indigenous people should be treated. The industry, if it cares, will have to regulate itself. And if it doesn't care, then some outside environmentally-concerned group will have to do what it can. In the meantime consider the second proposal:

b) Fixing of Lower Limit

There should be a lower limit under which a trekking agency cannot quote. The suggestion is that limit should be $35 per client per day. Only by charging the Western trekking agent that much money, can the Kathmandu agent hope to provide the proper service and to adequately pay the actual workforce. At the present time there is, in effect, a down-limit of $20 per day, because each trekker has to show that he spends $20 per day in Nepal before he can get his trekking permit. However, not all that money will be spent on his trek. But, for all intents and purposes, when it comes to taxation the Government assumes that each trekker represents an income of at least $20 per day to the trekking agent. It would help the situation if this amount was put up from $20 to $35 per day.

c) Trekking Agencies should Work Together

One reason that the Japanese have been successful business-men is because they choose to work with a supplier not because he is cheaper than another but because that supplier is willing to work with the parent company to the mutual advantage of the consumer by adaption and flexibility. They don't see each other as competitors. Similarly, that is how Western agents should seek to work with their suppliers—the foreign trekking agents in a commonality of interest to the benefit of the tourist and tourism. Western agents themselves could all benefit if they were to work together rather than the opposite. Rather than trying to score points over each other, and putting each other down, it would be better if we all helped each other—that would make for a better business all round. We could then apply concerted pressure on the Himalayan governments to reform the system of Liaison Officers.

If some, or all, of these proposals, are thought to have validity, and worthy of further development, then consider how they might be implemented.

d) *Endorsement of Proven Eco-Trekking Agents*
There are precedents in pressuring organisations and groups to modify the excesses of the market economy—take for instance, child abuse in the carpet manufacturing industry of India, now there is a move in the West to avoid buying such products. There is also the effect of public opinion on ivory purchase to the benefit of the elephant. The world has seen the effect on the racist South African Government of denying that country sporting and social contacts. We need a prestigious and reputable body here in Britain (Tourism Concern) and Europe to endorse those trekking companies that do not allow their agents abroad to exploit third-world labour. Similarly in the Himalaya there needs to be a creditable body which can give "the stamp of approval" to agents out there. This area might appeal to the hard-working organisers of A.C.A.P. (Annapurna Conservation Area Project) or K.E.E.P. (Kathmandu Environmental Education Project) and also to the editors of the excellent and essential *Himal* magazine based in Kathmandu.

e) *Pension Fund for Local Climbing and Trek Workers*
Just consider Per Temba, one of the finest Sherpa climbing Sirdars of the 70s and 80s, a man who has climbed Everest four times. The garage next door to his house in Kathmandu exploded in flame, Per Temba's house caught fire—he lost everything, with no comeback on the garage and no help from anyone, but self-help and help from his Sherpa friends. Now he is in his mid-forties and beginning to worry about what will happen to him when he can no longer climb mountains and has not the strength to go on treks. There is no government pension fund. What if he, or members of his family, become ill? These are matters which are worrying Per Temba. What about all the other Sherpas—those less well-known, such as Nima Tenzing who is now in his 60s and been on many an expedition? In fact, he was with Charles Evans in 1955 and on Kangchenjunga in 1979 for the third ascent, and conducted tourists along Himalayan valleys year after year, until this year. He is just

too old to go trekking so he stays at home, hiring out his few yaks to trekking agents going past his home to Everest Base Camp. He can eke out a living at that, but he has six daughters and no sons—big dowries and less and less land. A group of Nima Tenzing's friends are contributing for a donation towards his retirement, but that is hardly satisfactory—it is very hit and miss. The Sherpas have always been nomadic at heart and entrepreneurs, playing the field and going from one trekking agency to another. There needs to be a provident scheme in Khumbu, run by themselves. A trust for the benefit of elderly Sherpas under the trusteeship of the Sherpa people and may be co-opted outsiders who have the Sherpas' welfare very much at heart. There is a lot that needs doing, here and in other areas of Nepal and the Himalaya.

f) *Everyday Demands of the Trekking Unions*

In sheer frustration, several trekking unions sprang up during the first year of democracy in Nepal, to protect the interests of those working in the trekking industry. Some of these unions, out of sheer frustration, were quite radical. The Trekking Workers' Association of Nepal (TWAN) put 77 demands in front of the Minister of Tourism.

Whilst not all of these recommendations would appeal to Westerners, and indeed not to every Nepalese, some of them did seem to be sensible and have been voiced many times before, such as discouraging foreign group leaders operating in Nepal to ensure more work for indigenous leaders. The porters and staff must be supplied with adequate food and clothing and shelter by the local trekking agents so they can perform their labours safely. They should also be trained in such specialist activities as using crampons and ascending and descending ropes. The majority of the demands were to safeguard the welfare of the labourers in the trekking business. At the present time labour conditions are quite Dickensian.

Decline of Cultural Heritage due to Advancing Tourism

There is no doubt that the observer will change the object of his observations just by passing by. All the local people will become curious, and more so, the more people they see from the

West, in their fancy clothing, carrying expensive cameras, tape recorders and Walkmans, being waited on hand and foot by their own kind. Curiosity is roused, the young people become unsettled and their material expectations will rise; they will eventually be lured down to Kathmandu away from the village and fields, which puts pressure on those who remain—the womenfolk. The old customs and crafts are forgotten and old traditions are overtaken by the marketplace.

The trekkers' demand for local produce inflates the cost, and, in effect, puts a lot of that produce out of the reach of the poorer people.

It is hard to gauge the cheapening effect of tourism, of foreigners descending on the village, peering into houses, may be settling down for the day with tape-recorder and interpreter recording intimate details of family life. Forever the click of cameras, and if it isn't tourists, it's sociologists, anthropologists, economists, etc. etc. They say of the Eskimo that every Eskimo has a harpoon, his kayak, his sledge and his anthropologist. The same may be said of the Sherpa people who are inundated by people conducting surveys on their history and lifestyle. How much change do we want, or rather how much change do they want, or how many tourists do they want to visit their valleys?

Well the buzz word now in Khumbu and most of Nepal is "quality" tourism rather than "quantity" tourism. That is to move generally in the direction of tourism as it is practised in Bhutan. There the King, his monks and ministers are working to bring Bhutan more gradually into the modern age than has happened in Nepal. Having seen what they consider to be the harmful effects of tourism on the cultural heritage of Nepal, they have decided to restrict tourism to about 2500 people per year. They have done that by charging $250 for every day the tourist is in their country. They, therefore, have some of the benefits of tourism without having too many of the adverse side-effects. It works for them, and it works well for the tourist—at least for those who can afford to go there. If we regard it as a privilege, which it is, and worth saving for, then that might help. Don't let us forget that only forty years ago, no one ever went to Nepal, it was totally cut-off to foreigners. There are restrictions in Bhutan, there are restrictions in Tibet, and, may be, there have to be restrictions in Nepal—on the number of tourists and regulations as to how much those who do go contribute financially. May be the lone traveller has to be a thing of the past so that no one can travel around Nepal without his "guide". He doesn't have to be a guide so much as a local companion. It will still be a fantastic individual experience.

The interventionist policies outlined above will not immediately appeal to everyone. Even at the height of the Thatcher years the economy in Britain was regulated. There can never be a total free-for-all approach. Freedom requires that we accept responsibilities and that there should be eternal vigilance otherwise the unscrupulous will take advantage and monopolise that freedom.

(Kurt Diemberger)

1. Tons of material are brought in every year to the Baltoro glacier (Karakoram) by hundreds of porters.

(Kurt Diemberger)

2. K2 and waste on the glacier (1987). The clean up expedition by 'Mountain Wilderness' drew international attention to the problem.

(A. Soncini) (Archives: Kurt Diemberger)

3. Burning waste and carrying away remnants (with camels in the background).
'Mountain Wilderness' in action; Shaksgam, China.

(Chris Bonington)

4. Rubbish at Base Camp at Nanga Parbat.

Verpackung
für Expediti ...
Deutsches Instit...
...dsforschung
Leitung: Prof. Dr. Herrligkoffer
8000 München ...

5. Rubbish at Base Camp at Nanga Parbat.

(Chris Bonington)

(Kurt Diemberger)

6. Wood to fuel climbing and trekking. Everest area Khumbu, 1978, Nepal.

(Kurt Diemberger)

7. Wood-porters carrying out of the Karmachu forest, Tibet.

(Harish Kapadia)

8. Remains of forest fire. A fire started by a careless trekking group in Nepal.

(R.D. Bhattacharji)

9. Abondoned bunker on a seemingly unsullied plain on the Indus, Ladakh.
Many such permanent human habitations by the security forces threaten environment.

(R.D. Bhattacharji)

10. The Tamarisk Bush in Rupshu, southeast Ladakh. This is the first to
attract attention and to be attacked by the trekkers as it burns well.

11. Everyone is no better! Mass post emotion and sublimeness or the Matterhorn

(Kurt Diemberger)

Poverty and Himalayan Development

BRIG. D.K. KHULLAR (Retd.)

Brigadier Khullar has been on a dozen major Himalayan expeditions, mostly as the leader. These have included the Indian Everest Expedition, 1984, which placed the first Indian woman, Bachendri Pal, on the summit, and a highly successful Joint Indo-British Army Expedition to Saser Kangri via the difficult West Ridge—a first. He was the Principal of the Himalayan Mountaineering Institute, Darjeeling from 1981 to 1985.

M y premise is that ours is by and large either the exploiter's or in other cases the sophisticate's view point of the situation in the Himalaya. One wonders why doesn't one hear of cries like 'Save the Alps'[1] etc. How many of us have cared to ask the local people inhabiting the Himalaya as to what they think of it all and how best they can help the cause and themselves in the first place? I am afraid many of us go around with superior and condescending attitudes. For many of us it would be an anathema if the locals were to lose their primitive customs, dress and living habits. They are so exotic, part of the flora and fauna package for the tourist who comes after spending many thousands of dollars to watch them as he also comes to watch the Adivasi and the tigers of Ranthambore in the Indian mainland.

The truth is that modernisation has already made some in-roads

---

1. 'One wonders why doesn't one hear of cries like "Save the Alps", etc.' One does indeed; every Alpine Club, dozens of environmental associations utter these cries and are active in trying to protect the Alps from further degradation—Ed.

into the Himalaya and very soon will spread further. I am sure that even the people living in far distant valleys and high altitude regions would like to have modern amenities: excellent roads, electricity, running water, schools, colleges, hospitals and other civil institutions. So far whatever has happened is shoddy and ill planned. The reasons are obvious. The Himalaya are part of the developing countries which is an euphemism for basically poor nations. The local people themselves are not being involved in affairs that should concern them most. The greatest industry with potential in the Himalaya is tourism but who is making the money and benefiting by it? It is the tour operator. The Himalayan environment is only peripheral in his scheme of things. Added to all this is the atrocious sense of public hygiene and sanitation of our people of the Indian subcontinent.

As I have written earlier, why is there no cry of 'Save the Alps'? Why is Switzerland so beautiful in spite of it receiving a million more tourists than the Himalayan states put together and in spite of the fact that you can reach the top of Mont Blanc in a cable car as also all other favourite sites for skiing and mountaineering.[2] It is because Switzerland is a very rich country and its people are also very rich. Nepal these days is literally permitting a stampede on the summit of Everest much to the chagrin of the puritans. They would probably put up a cable car if they could raise the money. In the final analysis therefore it's all a question of economics. I think the solution for the protection of the Himalaya lies in improving the economy of the people living there and by involving them. It must be understood that roads and dams would continue to be built deeper and deeper into the Himalaya, deforestation as well as afforestation will take place, the crowding and littering of rubbish in the more popular and easily accessible resorts will increase. It's all bad news for the old Himalayan hands. The world is now an over-explored place and this includes the Himalaya. The solution lies in making the best of the situation and channelising the flow of modernisation in a positive aggressive manner. Let the governments,

---

2. 'In spite of the fact that you can reach the top of Mont Blanc in a cable car'. No, not quite. There is no téléphérique or railway which goes to within 1000 m of the summit—Ed.

the World Bank and other organisations help to build new villages and relocate some of the existing ones. Let there be large scale afforestation. Let them line the roads with trees, perennials and set up facilities like toilets, bathrooms and cafeterias at convenient places en route. Let us enforce laws on public hygiene and sanitation vigorously and resolutely. Let the cleaning up itself be a profit-making income-generating activity involving the private entrepreneur. It is a bogey that all concrete structures are ugly and eco-hostile; not these days when we have some excellent expertise in landscaping. Let there be greater spread of education and health care and let the local economy get a real boost so that the people acquire the requisite motivation and pride in keeping their areas clean. It's not an impossible task specially when the Himalaya is so thinly populated compared to the rest of the Indian subcontinent. It's all a question of education, landscaping and providing opportunities. The potential is simply tremendous.

I am afraid I have not touched the micro issues. These I feel are inconsequential and would be taken care of in case the economic miracle in the Himalaya can be ushered in. Of course movements that cry halt to the various depredations let loose by the money-baggers, and thoughtless and corrupt officials must carry on relentlessly and I am all for them.

The Impact of Tourism

ISOBEL SHAW

Isobel Shaw is a tourism consultant to the Government of Pakistan and a tour guide specializing in the mountains of Central Asia. She is the author of five guides to Pakistan including the *Pakistan Trekking Guide*, 1993.

She has sent us the text of her talk on 'The Impact of Tourism on Life in Mountain Villages in Gilgit and Baltistan in Northern Pakistan.' It was given with slides, to the British Mountaineering Council Conference on the Impact on the Environment and Social Development of Mountain Related Tourism in the Greater Ranges, 25 May 1993. Extracts are given below

K 2 and the four other 8000 m peaks (Nanga Parbat, Broad Peak and Gasherbrums I and II) attract more climbers and trekkers than anywhere else in northern Pakistan. You can fly directly from Islamabad to Gilgit or Skardu, or get there via the Karakoram Highway.

The Hunza valley is more developed than the Skardu region because about one third of the population along the Hunza river is Ismaili—that is followers of the Aga Khan, the most liberal sect of Islam. The Baltistan people are less advanced than in Hunza, less educated, mainly because a majority of the people are strict Shia Muslims.

These valleys were isolated until 1978 when the Karakoram Highway opened along the Indus and Hunza rivers linking Pakistan with China. New jeep roads to the top of almost every side valley have opened the whole area to trade and tourism.

The area is changing fast because of the road, tourism and the population explosion. The population in the northern areas (and in Pakistan as a whole) has tripled in the past forty years and is now about one million people, 30 per cent of whom are under 10 years old.

The pressure on agricultural land and on fuel is intolerable. The land has never been able to support the people. Until 1892, the main source of income was from raiding the trade caravans. Now it is essential to develop tourism to supplement the economies of these mountain villages. The Karakoram Highway enables men to migrate in search of work.

Tourism is the fastest growing industry. But more of the money generated by tourism must stay with the local people. At the moment most expeditions bring almost everything with them from their home country. This is expensive for the expedition and does not benefit the mountain people enough.

The people of the Karakoram are jumping at the dream of money to be made through tourism. They want jobs as porters and guides. They are keen to build extra rooms for guests or small rest houses or little hotels. The locals need advice and training. There are government agencies and non-governmental organisations that run various projects in the area. Most prominent among these is the Aga Khan Foundation which has a large development project, the Aga Khan Rural Support Programme (AKRSP).

The AKRSP starts by encouraging the villagers to form organisations and have weekly meetings, to save collectively, put their money in the bank, and to plan development projects such as building roads and irrigation channels for the benefit of the whole village. (About 27 thousand hectares of newly irrigated land has been brought into use.) The AKRSP gives loans for these projects using the village's savings as collateral, while the actual savings continue to earn interest in the bank.

The tourism developments that are most noticeable to the

visitor are the hotels and other new buildings. Cement is replacing the traditional style everywhere. The first priority in tourism development is to keep the area beautiful. Tourists are attracted to a place because it is beautiful. They go to the northern areas of Pakistan for the mountains and the cultural interest—the traditional way of life, the costumes, the customs, the architecture. The people here have been isolated for a long time. To them cement is modern and gives status. They need advice on how to develop the area but keep its traditional identity. The Aga Khan Trust for Culture is encouraging appropriate development by offering incentives in the form of loans and grants to those who build in keeping with the traditional style.

Another huge problem is fuel. Three million trees are planted each year in the northern area. And in the 15 years since I first went to Hunza, you can really see the difference. Expeditions can help here by supplying all fuel necessary for their porters and forbidding them to cut wood.

Many mountaineers go to the mountains with their mind fixed on their goal, their summit. They often give little thought to their host country or the people who live there or what they can offer in return for their visit. They could use their time to educate as much as possible by example.

Some Effects of Tourism

Villagers are keeping fewer animals than before. They no longer have the manpower to take the herds to the high pastures in summer. The pastures furthest from the villages are no longer used. Those nearest to the villages, where the women alone can take the herds, are overgrazed.

When the men are working away from the village, the women have to do extra work, but this has some good side effects. It gives the women the chance to make more of the decisions on the land, what crops to grow, when to plant and harvest. It also gives them some control of the household money.

Tooth decay from sweets and biscuits given by tourists is

becoming a problem. The mountain people have no access to dentists.

Tourism encourages the commercialisation and distortion of local cultures. But the cultures are bound to change anyway with the opening of the roads. Nothing is static. In fact tourism can preserve local culture in some form by showing interest in tradition. Local ceremonies will be 'refined'—changed for tourists, a fee charged, and the ceremonies performed to order. This may distress the anthropologists, but on the other hand it does preserve a culture that is dying anyway. Otherwise old ballads, dances and music, the planting and harvesting ceremonies, might be lost completely. It might be better to revive the ceremonies for the tourists than lose them altogether.

The First Priorities
— Keep the mountains beautiful to attract tourists
— Encourage appropriate building
— Encourage more tree planting
— Substitute other fuels for wood such as hydro-electric, kerosene, solar and bottled gas.
— The National Parks need to be run on the Zimbabwe lines with locals used as guards and guides and locals reaping the benefits of any income from hunting and fishing licences. The national parks as they are set up now just do not work. People's grazing land has been confiscated without compensation. They see no return from the parks and no point in them.
— Local people are the key factor, they must have a say in the planning of their own future.

Help by Mountaineering Expeditions
— By ensuring that a greater proportion of income from tourism stays in the area.
— By using local porters and guides
— Western mountaineering schools could develop local guide training schemes. The French are already doing this, but they offer the training in summer, at peak tourist season when none of the guides are free. The courses should be in

the winter for maximum participation. But winter is peak season in Europe when the European guides are busy.

— Expeditions should buy as much produce as possible in the area—cereals, fruit, vegetables and meat. I have published precise lists of what food and fuel is available in Gilgit, Skardu and Chitral (see *Pakistan Trekking Guide,* Odyssey, Hong Kong 1993). The BMC could keep these lists upto-date and encourage expeditions to use them, and not take everything with them from home.

— Tourists could buy embroidered handicrafts and take them home as presents. Most of the old handicrafts, except the hats, are now only produced for tourist consumption. Tourism keeps the old handicrafts alive and provides an extra income for the women.

— Tourists should not give sweets and biscuits or 'one pen' to the children.

— Try not to encourage begging.

— Do not contaminate the village water supplies.

One of the first things future expeditions can do to help the economies of the northern areas of Pakistan is to spread the load more evenly. Everyone is dazzled by the five 8000 m peaks in Pakistan.

This year (1993) 77 expeditions have been given mountaineering permits to Pakistan. Of these, 42 are going up the Baltoro Glacier to Concordia to attempt K2, Broad Peak and the Gasherbrums 1, 2 and 4. Eleven are going to Nanga Parbat. Only two are going to the whole of the Hindukush one to Tirich Mir and one to Istoro Nal.

There are over a hundred 7000 m peaks in Pakistan. So why not chose one of these, have a great uncrowded climb, and thus spread the load? And let's try to set a good example and make a real active effort to clear up our garbage. Here it is the tourists and mountaineers who need the training.

The Sanctity of the Himalaya

S.P. GODREJ

Soli Godrej has loved mountaineering. Some of the most exhilarating and memorable hours in his earlier days were linked with high-level climbing in Kashmir and Nepal. He recalls trekking in the mid-forties 28 miles and 20 miles on two successive days from Sonmarg to the Zoji La and back and then on to Amarnath and back to Baltal the next day. Godrej also indulged in this favourite activity in the Swiss Alps and a bit in the Andes and Rockies, apart from walking up to the summit of Kilimanjaro.

He has been a member of the Himalayan Club from 1978. Mountaineering, to him, promotes the spirit of adventure, extends consciousness about the threatened environment, stimulates tourist interest, particularly adventure tourism. Above all, mountaineering has given him spiritual satisfaction.

Mountaineering has always fascinated me. Not only because in my salad days I was keen on mountaineering myself, but because I believe that mountaineering expeditions tend to stimulate tourist interest. I have, almost all my life, advocated the manifold benefits of tourism—including the multiplier effect. Presently tourism is the largest foreign exchange earner, but we earn only a fraction of what even very small countries earn because of our weak infrastructure and lack of awareness among our people of the benefits of tourism, especially adventure tourism, but even more because such expeditions are an extension of our consciousness about the threatened environment.

It was for these reasons that we, in Godrej, were happy to be associated in May-June 1992 with the highly successful Panch Chuli Expedition led by the legendary Chris Bonington with Harish Kapadia as co-leader.

Difficult as it is to believe, the very remote and extensive region of the Himalaya, region of eternal snows and varied vegetation, is being ravaged today by environmental lapses. The situation became so grave that the Himalayan Environment Trust, an organisation of eminent mountaineers, was set up in 1988, and had to release a code of conduct for would-be mountaineers.

This code of conduct sets out rules to help keep camp sites clean and limit deforestation by not building open fires and avoiding the use of firewood. Other bits of advice include the burial of all bio-degradable material including food, to carry out all non-biodegradable litter, to remove rubbish wherever it may be found, to keep local water clean and avoid using pollutants, to nurture plants and desist from plucking them. The code also sets out other rules for foreign climbers, such as the reminder to take shoes off before entering temples and not to wear shorts or kiss or hold hands in public.

In preserving the Himalayan environment, we can also learn from efforts made to protect the Alpine environment. In October 1987, the Swiss Alpine Club appointed a permanent official to be responsible for all matters relating to the protection of the Alpine environment. Trying to protect the Alps has become a full-time battle, with the Club becoming a control point of information and contact, and ensuring continuity and availability so as to act in time to oppose any damaging project.

As in many other fields, there has been a population explosion in climbing, trekking and above all skiing. This is true of the Himalaya as of other mountain ranges. According to the *Himalayan Club Newsletter*, there are over 200 climbing expeditions a year, and innumerable trekkers both from abroad and from India. Thus, it is reported that the 'Spark' of Bangalore which began in 1981 with 15 members now has 6000. This is but one example among many.

We can therefore learn from the Alpine experience, as pointed out by Aamir Ali in the *Himalayan Club Newsletter*. Since the Himalaya cover eight countries, the International Centre for Integrated Mountain Development in Kathmandu could provide a framework. Failing this, the UN Environment Programme could be utilised to make a beginning with India, Bhutan and Nepal. It has been suggested that our Parliament could legislate designating different types of zones, those which should remain inviolate for the sole use of the snow leopard and the lammergeier, those in which climbing and trekking could be allowed in limited numbers in set conditions, and those where climbing, trekking and skiing could be encouraged.

While government regulations and interventions are necessary, it is private organisations that must play the major role in preparing a blue-print of measures like designating zones, protecting forests, setting up biosphere reserves, national parks and sanctuaries, making gas cylinders available, providing toilet facilities, and so on.

The most important consideration will be the disposal of garbage. Incinerators should be installed at designated points and expeditions should be encouraged to carry back hard garbage with them. Garbage should be transported to designated points from where it could be ferried by men or helicopters for disposal. Toilets in these high-density areas, as in the Alps where four types of toilets are installed in different huts, should be on the pit-compost system. A levy on visitors could help defray the expenses.

Degradation is one thing. Plunder of the region is quite another. It has been said that medicinal and aromatic herbs and plants which are nature's unique gifts at the height of 2500-3000 metres, are being systematically plundered by pharmaceutical houses of Bombay, Baroda and Delhi through agents and sub-agents who are also being robbed in the process. For example, these mountain folk may get upto Rs. 250/- for a kilo of roots and herbs after a week's gathering, which sells for as much as Rs. 2500/- per kilo when it reaches the metropolitan cities. Roots and rhizomes pulled out in the process stop further re-generation. The earth cover disappears, soil erosion begins and wildlife becomes extinct. Truly a heavy price to pay for human greed. Lack of discipline and awareness of the vital importance of conservation continue to harm our interests and prevent the resurgence of our nation.

Too many climbers are leaving behind too much trash. Soon there will be package ski-trips to the Himalaya, just as today there are package trekking expeditions. This will make the problems acuter. The solutions brook no delay, for to delay would be, both metaphorically and literally, a Himalayan blunder. As Carlo Alberto Pinelli. International Co-ordinator of Mountain Wilderness puts it: "It is necessary to develop the deep-rooted conviction that the ascent of a peak, or the opening up of a new route, or the realization of a sports achievement, lose their significance, if they are attained at the expense of the areas in question."

Above all, for unity and racial harmony we should adopt worship of all-embracing Mother nature. The Indian ethos is not complete without the inclusion of the sanctity of the Himalaya in all respects.

Some Do's and Don't's

Colonel Balwant S. Sandhu has had varied experience in the mountains including ascents of Changabang, Nanda Devi, Mamostang Kangri and White Water Running with noted Indian and international climbers for over 35 years.

He was Principal of the Nehru Institute of Mountaineering, Uttarkashi, and Adviser to the Indian Army for adventure activities. He is a past President of the Himalayan Club and a member of the American Alpine Club, Central Himalayan Environment Association (CHEA), Nainital, Jawahar Institute of Mountaineering and the Indian Mountaineering Foundation. Currently, he is Vice-President of this Foundation.

He was awarded the National Arjuna Award for excellence in mountaineering in 1983. He is deeply committed to the promotion of adventure and environmental awareness among the younger generation.

What do I consider the major environmental problems of the Himalaya?

1. Pollution of water by individuals out trekking; sewage by the ever-growing colonies of humans, government agencies, paramilitary and Bania settlements along the pilgrim routes; included are the labour camps for various projects such as road building. Hotels to be included.

2. Pollution by the above and by dams, cement factories and lime quarries of not only the water but of the air and the countryside. There isn't a reasonable wilderness area free of foil and

plastic bags. And noise pollution from vehicles and loud speakers.

3. Erosion from road building, human habitations and other human activity. I talk of avoidable erosion that comes with the attitude that the landscape belongs to nobody.

4. Absence of a 'Building Code' in the Himalaya: 'build where you like, as like, when you like,' appears to be the rule. With suitable planning, shelters for humans and machines could and must be found where these do not interfere with the drainage, do not pollute and are aesthetic.

5. Absence of a viable or effective authority to look out, spot wrong doers, act, eliminate the wrong and restore. I am sure reams of 'authority' lie amidst files and in the government offices and the jeeps flying about with the speed and vision of satyrs.

*How have we (my wife and me) dealt with questions of
garbage, toilets and fuel?*

6. *Garbage*: Do not throw it all over; bin it. Bio-degradable gets buried into the earth. Combustible—less the noisome plastics—are fired properly; tins, bottles are smashed and portered out to suitable dumps where these are recycled. And above all, sensible packaging cuts down garbage.

7. *Toilets*: Not by the water! Or by the trail or road; get off to deposit waste in a little depression and cover with rock and earth; use communal, natural or man-made holes in the alpine regions. This is important in areas of heavy use like camping grounds and Base Camps.

8. *Fuel*: Dress and eat sensibly to conserve body heat. Use kero oil or gas. In residential areas, construct sensibly (insulate and ventilate); use solar or wind power; use hot water bottles; do not let religious zealots trade 'hot' springs.

*What practical measures do I suggest to deal with the
problem of the degradation of the Himalayan environment?*

9. Our problem is the human (including his animal and machine) who for survival, livelihood and profit pollutes the environment. Educate (start with schools in the plains!) about the control

of pollution. Fine heavily and those unable to pay the fine must give their time.

10. Do not terminate roads where the carrying capacity will be exceeded; stop short and build pedal cycles, footpaths. Build hotels (dhabas) well off the roads and tracks. Tea stalls and shops should be sited where they are not seen from the roads and tracks. Settle for tented camps, mountain huts in suitable places. Instant fines, entered in the 'trade' book for a first offence against the environment, heavier ones for repeats. Similar 'highhandedness' against the trekker, pilgrim or driver or other visitor. Fine for being seen chewing gum or spitting it in any public place in Singapore is, I believe, $50.

11. Treat the entire Himalaya like somebody's garden: only then will you see or spot a digger or a builder or a wood cutter. Stop him, fine him. Like they do in Europe, Japan, Singapore, or I believe in Bhutan and the US. Long time ago the wise man Moses said it for you and me to repeat: those who do not live by these rules must die by these rules. We know the shepherd must cut trees, must build, must pollute our water because he does it for his survival. Perhaps what we do not know is that the entire herd belongs to a rich *Bania* or politician or a Thakur, living in the MLA flats in Lucknow, for example. The problem is not of abject poverty but of reaching the vested interests.

12. A single visible authority, call it by any name, to be effective in the Himalaya. This authority must not be burdened with venal subordinate staff: just officers, not unlike Game Wardens, like say in the Gangotri region, these would be the principals—past and present, all class 1 gazetted officers, officers of the forest, wild life, PWD etc. alternatively, a Highway Authority to take care of the environmental cancer along the highways. The officers must spend 1/3 of the month out walking!

13. And lastly, to reduce pressure on some areas, trans-valley routes like Gangotri-Kalindikhal-Mana; Govind Ghat-Bhuyandar-Ghamsali; Harsil-Lamkhaga-Chitkul etc. ought to be blazed, so a lay trekker need not fear crossing one of these. This also entails easy availability of accurate walking maps and reliable, light-weight camping gear.

Mountain Clubs and Education

KURT DIEMBERGER

Kurt Diemberger was on the 1957 successful Austrian expedition to Broad Peak with Hermann Buhl, an early Alpine style climb with no high altitude porters. He was with Buhl again on Chogolisa when Buhl disappeared; he climbed Dhaulagiri in 1960 and went on to climb several other 8000ers.

Having been asked by the Austrian Alpine Club for a contribution with some ideas for the symposium, here they are.

What are the major environmental problems of the Himalaya?

These are on the one hand caused by the enormously increased numbers of visitors—be it trekkers, other tourists or expeditions. On the other hand by the increasing number of locals who live in this environment and use it (think for example of firewood or of mountain slopes being transformed into fields). By regulations on the one side and education of both visitors and locals for a better understanding of the problems, it is possible to help to some extent regarding environmental protection, but even then the main handicap is the increasing numbers.

Dealing with garbage, toilets and fuel

Our mountain clubs already have taken strong interest by influence on, and when possible, education of their members to protect the mountain environment, and I got the impression that a general consciousness regarding garbage is on its way, that mountaineers and trekkers widely use gas or other stoves (but much less so with their porter crew) and that groups usually make toilet holes. But the spiritual influence is hard to dam and many visitors will certainly change the social structure of a place. In my eyes, the real problem is not the garbage, even if I agree it is a good deed to get rid of it.

Practical measures to deal with these problems

* Cleaning expeditions—as for instance the Mountain Wilderness 'Free K2' expedition 1990, led by C.A. Pinelli.
* Fees for such purpose.
* Governmental decision, where the garbage can be dumped or brought for recycling.
* Restrictions against deforestation—and the planting of new trees.
* Creation of National Parks.
* Promotion of small expeditions—if, as an example, only four persons go to climb an eight thousander, there should be a discount of 50% on the present royalty for them—small enterprises do really need promotion; big ones, who also put more burden on the environment, have usually enough money anyway.
* Environmental education hours for visitors, while in the area. And for locals, at school, and when portering.
* Restricted areas of wilderness to be entered only with a special permit.
* Severe restrictions against helicopter—transport of trekkers, mountaineers or other visitors to Himalayan or Karakoram base camps, cutting the approach march with its fatigue (see the UIAA decision against such a project 1993, regarding K2 from the China side).

Whatever action cuts or diminishes the "barrier of fatigue" will result in a strong increase of visitors and thus increase the main problem.

Protecting the Cultural Environment

MANMOHAN SINGH BAWA

Manmohan Singh Bawa is a member of the Himalayan Club. He owns a hotel at Dalhousie and alternates between Dalhousie and New Delhi. He has trekked extensively in the Himalaya. He published excellent sketch-maps of the entire Himalayan range, which were well received by trekkers.

The Himalaya for the last few years have been the focus of environmentalists who fear that its delicate eco-balance is being disturbed. In our opinion, besides the well known problems such as deforestation, soil erosion and the like, the invisible and therefore more dangerous problem is the pollution of indigenous culture and its surrounding environment in the Himalaya. The main cause behind this is the increase in adventure tourism in the area along with the increase in 'yatris' to the pilgrim centres and the construction and extension of roads deep into the Himalaya.

There is no doubt that tourism in Himalaya attracts foreign tourists and trekkers into the country bringing with them valuable foreign exchange. It also provides employment to a number of people, the local population being a minor and incidental beneficiary of this. The major portion of the profit is pocketed by the tourist agencies, equipment manufacturers and ancilliary service agencies.

Few years ago, Bhutan had invited a team of specialists on Himalayan tourism, who suggested that Bhutan with its high peaks and monasteries and picturesque landscape had high potential for attracting international tourists. Fortunately, wisdom dawned upon the tiny State and they realised the negative influence which this tourism would have on its monks/monasteries, tradition and on the culture of the indigenous people. Instead of falling prey to the lure of foreign exchange, they shelved the report and while not forbidding tourism, have not made it so easy that dilettantes too can access the country and contribute to a culture invasion from the outside.

It is not the small trekking parties of a few individuals who go to the mountains with a genuine interest in trekking and culture but the money grabbing tourist agents who pose the most potent threat to the hill people. Their clients, the rich of the rich countries, walk through the villages of the poorest of the poor, exhibiting their expensive clothes and gadgetry. It is not unusual for the agents to organise so-called cultural events that call upon the local men and women to provide dance performances for the 'real' and 'authentic' entertainment of their clients, thus prostituting the local culture and degrading its people to the lowest level. We have all encountered children on these routes begging for toffees and money and we all know who has taught them to beg. These children are the most visible manifestation of the pollution of the Himalaya.

The influx of foreigners is followed by idol thieves who, with the help of some tourist agents, corrupt the local inhabitants with the glitter of their money and smuggle priceless works of art out of India. The theft of the idols from Kamru fort in Sangla Valley is an example at hand.

We firmly believe that material prosperity (usually limited to a few) can not be equated with development. In fact, it robs the area of its inherent social and cultural balance. The claim that adventure tourism in the Himalaya has brought about an increase in the standard of living of the local inhabitants is a myth. The only change that has come about is that it has transformed them from contented farmers to dissatisfied porters, with the vices of the city people.

River rafting, too, has contributed its share to polluting the banks of some rivers. Unfortunately, the rafting exercises are concentrated on particular stretches of certain rivers only. The stretch between Manali and Bhuntar is a case in point. Hundreds of empty tin cans, polythene bags and other leftovers can be seen littering the banks of the Beas river.

The worst type of damage to the environment is caused by large-scale pilgrimages in the Himalaya. The continuous need of wood for fuel and buildings have left the Himalayan slopes bare of trees so that if one was to travel from Rishikesh to Badrinath, one would rarely see a Deodar tree adorning the hills around. Similarly, the Hemkund area has started attracting hundreds and thousands of Sikh pilgrims and we are afraid that the beautiful valley of Bhuinder Ganga will turn barren in a few years. While all the filth and human excreta pollute the waters of the Ganga and other rivers, plastic bags are seen clinging to the bushes on the slopes like ugly scars.

Twenty years ago, the number of visitors to the Mani Mahesh fair in the Chamba valley was a few hundred. Five years ago it was twenty thousand. This year it was more than one lakh. Most of the visitors camp for the night and relieve themselves in the morning in the catchment area of the Mani Mahesh lake; the result is that it turns into a huge public toilet. This waste gets deposited in the bed of the lake. The same is the case of Hanuman Chatti, where during the *yatra* season one can see thousands of pilgrims squatting on the banks of the river and on both sides of the road itself.

As the roads cut through the mountains, the forest contractors trucks also go along with them. With the connivance of the forest officials and the local politicians, the contractor's axe fells trees mercilessly leaving denuded slopes. Thirty years ago, the slopes from Palchan to Marhi on the Manali-Rohtang Pass route were densely forested with gigantic deodar trees. Now only a few of these trees survive. On the other hand, it is the local inhabitants who perpetrate the least harm to the environment to which they have adapted their needs. On our trek from Helang to Kalpeshwar, we were told that the inhabitants of the area were not allowing the construction of a road to their village because they feared the depredation of their forests by outsiders. The results of deforestation are too well-known to be enumerated here.

It is a shame that the majority of so called great mountaineers of India have chosen to become travel agents thus contributing to the pollution of the cultural heritage and the lives of the people of the Himalaya while paying lip service to environmental protection in public fora.

There is no ready-made solution to these problems. The lure of money and *moksha* are going to defeat any effort made in this direction. Certain suggestions are given below:

* New areas in the Himalaya should not be opened to foreigners.
* Trekking/tourist agencies should be made more responsible.
* Tourist agencies should not concentrate on a few chosen routes; instead their activities should be spread to many different areas and trails.

Trash and the Himalayan Expedition

LINDSAY GRIFFIN

Lindsay Griffin is a well-known mountaineer living in the
Wales, has climbed various ranges and high peaks. At
present, he is the editor of the 'Mountain Info' in *High*,
covering mountaineering activities the world over.

We all realise that the solution to the problem of litter lies simply in education: what may be unsightly litter to one person or one nation, may pass unnoticed to another.

The well-known incident concerning a British team at an overnight camping spot on the approach march to Concordia is a good example of misconception. The designated campsite was particularly squalid, with copious amounts of rubbish from previous groups. Through the Sirdar, the leader organised the porters each with a large bag, and asked them to walk in line across the site collecting all the litter and eventually tipping it into a pile near to one corner of the area, where it would be burnt. The porters duly did as they were asked and at the end of their work all ceremoniously emptied the contents of their bags onto the proposed incineration site. The result was a huge pile of twigs; the western 'litter' lay untouched on the ground.

Whilst ensuring that there is an adequate number of porters at the end of any expedition to evacuate all the trash that cannot be successfully disposed of by proper burning or burying, secrecy should still be the word. Many a local porter would find it incomprehensible to realise that he was being paid to carry out a sack full of rubbish, and on a number of well-meaning expeditions the trash has never made it out to its intended destination.

A second, closely related problem is packaging. There is a very laudable tradition amongst expeditions to donate any unwanted goods remaining at the end of the trip to local helpers from the area. Most of the local people in Himalayan regions have little concept of packaging and expeditions should be very wary of giving away any excess food or equipment that is packaged in non-bio-degradable materials such as plastic, polythene, aluminium foil etc.

There are critics of large commercially organised expeditions who feel that the participants have less incentive when it comes to proper collection and disposal of trash. Whether this is correct or not, and I suspect that in general it is the latter, it is true that large expeditions (and traditionally notorious were those from the former Eastern Bloc countries) must take most of the blame. Having taken part in both large and small expeditions, I fully realise that even with the best will in the world it is considerably more difficult for a large team to monitor its waste disposal.

Small teams, which in turn require a small number of local helpers, can travel to and climb on their mountain with minimal impact on the environment, and most do. Those who do not have little excuse.

Any environmentally aware government should be heeding the current UIAA plea to stop discouraging small, light-weight expeditions by imposing heavy financial burdens, and look to the future rather than the (very) short-term benefits.

Echoing a Himalayan Concern

SUDHIR SAHI

Sudhir Sahi has been on many mountaineering expeditions and trekking routes in the Himalaya. He had been the Delhi Secretary of the Himalayan Club 1974-1992, and is a member of the Alpine and the American Alpine Clubs. He is the Honorary Secretary of the Indian Mountaineering Foundation (IMF), represents it on the Youth Commission of the International Union of Alpinist Associations, and edits its journal *Indian Mountaineer.*

He is also a member of the Himalayan Tourism Advisory Board, and of the Committee for Environmental Impact Assessment for Tourism and Transport Projects.

He has sent the following article which was first published in the *Indian Mountaineer*, No. 27, 1991.

Quicker access to distant locations, larger disposable incomes and an increased concern for the quality of life characterizes the large numbers of upmarket holiday seekers today. Matching this are the numerous adventure tourism options in India which provide leisure outlets for an unusual wilderness experience in the mountains, rivers, forests or on the beaches of the subcontinent.

By their very nature such destinations are environmentally fragile, their attractiveness being endangered by ingress well above the viable carrying capacity and large scale felling of trees for energy needs. It is, therefore, necessary to ensure attention to ecological safeguards so that the raison d'être of these areas becoming adventure tourism destinations is not lost.

We know that when the balance between natural processes is

subjected to heavy pressure, the damage so done can create irreversible positions whereby weather patterns and lifestyles· are thrown out of gear. Burning of fossil fuels and the resultant green house effect has led to global warming while the use of non-biodegradable containers such as aerosols has led to thinning of the protective ozone shield, thus raising ultraviolet radiation.

With reference to the Himalaya, the growth in trekking and mountaineering traffic is best illustrated by some plain statistics. In 1953, when Mount Everest was first climbed, there were less than 12 expeditions and 100 trekkers. The position today is that there are approximately 300 mountaineering expeditions and over 100,000 trekkers every year. One of the immediate consequences of this has been overcrowding of certain routes and their main bases such as the Khumbu Glacier at the base of Mount Everest and the Baltoro Glacier at the foot of K-2. While this is no doubt cause for concern, there is hope in that the set of experiences and corrective measures initiated in the European Alps is available. While permanent cures are strictly not available, timely action can help reduce the gravity of the problem. Essentially this involves the adoption (and, if necessary, enforcement) of ecological practices such as:

* trekking/mountaineering teams bringing in their own kerosene;
* removal of garbage for being burnt at the point of origin and not merely at the roadhead;
* purchase of food and supplies entirely at the point of origin so as not to strain availability at high altitude where material has to be transported at great cost; and above all
* limitations on team size with respect to the carrying capacity of the area.

In its recently released Fact Sheet series, the Centre for Science and Environment has listed the relevant provisions in the Constitution of India wherein (i) Article 48-A states that the State shall endeavour to protect and improve the environment and to safeguard the forests and wildlife of the country, and (ii) Article 51-A states that it shall be the duty of every citizen of India: to protect and improve the natural environment including forests, lakes, rivers and wildlife, and to have compassion for living creatures.

As the geographical area is vast, the expression of environmental concern depends largely on enlightened voluntary groups and the media. For this effort, the adventure tourism client is an effective target. There has also been demonstrable government intent for the adoption of appropriate technology. Thus in its remote Mustang district, Nepal has recently installed a windpower station using the high velocity sweep down the Kali Gandaki gorge at the foot of Annapurna and Dhaulagiri. With 15,000 trekkers visiting this area annually, the provision of electricity, albeit cumbersome, will reduce timbering for fuel. Moreover, this process is less inefficient than hydropower which is susceptible to seismic and flash flood dangers. Concerted effort is likewise under way for stemming pollution in the Jhelum river and the freshwater lakes of the Kashmir Valley. Lower down the ecological pyramid, similar attention is valid for afforestation, effluent discharge reduction for the rivers and attention to the high tide mark for construction near the beaches.

The situation could be viewed with reference to three kinds of broadly demarcated zones. The first of these might be an ecological inner line, as proposed by the noted observer Aamir Ali, beyond which human ingress is completely forbidden. Be it a long-term or a short-term embargo, as in the case of Nanda Devi Sanctuary, its aim would be to correct a grave ecological disturbance. The second broad zone could be one in which limited inflow is permitted with cautious supervision of visitor impact such as, for example, trails like the Kuari Pass and the Synthan and Margan Passes. The third broad zone could be one where carrying capacities have been analysed and, with adequate sanitation and disposal safeguards, there is relatively unrestricted movement of visitors. It needs hardly any emphasis that non-conventional energy sources must be used.

One of the key areas of concern in such a programme is training of personnel. These include the forest department, para-military border organisations and tourism industry representatives with direct field responsibility. Above all, a periodic review of ecological safeguards, emphasis on voluntary controls for sanitation and hygiene and use of bio-degradable packing materials will have to be encouraged. Publication of clear guidelines for adventure tour operators, outfitters, other suppliers and the actual client will go a long way in the adoption of operational norms. Simultaneously, itinerary design must take cognisance of these needs. Again, coordinated input for appropriate technological investment has to be planned in order to reduce the acceptance gap between the local population and its opinion leaders on the one hand and the trekking and other adventure groups visiting the wilderness areas on the other.

Guidelines for Environmental Action

ASPIE D. MODDIE

Aspie Moddie is a former President of the Himalayan Club and has been on many Himalayan expeditions. He has been active in environmental questions for some twenty years and has played an important part in turning the Club's attention to the need for protecting the Himalaya. The article given below is a slightly modified version of the guidance he provided to the Himalayan Environment Trust (HET).

A s one who has been rubbing his nose on the rock of Himalayan eco-development for 20 years, from the macro of the founding of ICIMOD, (International Centre for Integrated Mountain Development), to the micro of practical projects for the sustainable eco-development of two micro watersheds in the Kumaon region, I may be excused in beginning with three negative pre-conditions for proposed work in future, especially as they are bluntly expressed in the style of a mountain man.

Negative Pre-Conditions

1. First, as climbers and trekkers, if you are serious about mountain ecology, cease being mere birds of passage. Far from having any biological value, your unbiodegradeable droppings are a mounting ecological threat to the mountains and to mountain people. Edmund Hillary's example in the field of education and health—resulting in a cultural change in Solo Khumbu—is an admirable example of the opposite, sustainable involvement. Without which, even a one-time clean-up expedition is only a temporary palliative.

2. Stop talking in easy, bald generalisations at high-level, 5-star seminars. They do not cut much ice. I have seen these for 17 years and they still leave you with the question on the ground, "How to get started?" Realities on the ground are a world apart. Rub your nose against those realities on specifics on a micro-scale, as in mountain climbing. Nature can be hard enough; the complex combination of man and nature in eco-systems can be as formidable as the Eiger face itself, and it will take years to climb. There will be no summit.

3. Avoid eco-tourism. It's pleasant. It's self-righteous. It too cuts no ice.

Self-Questioning and Answers

HET or any such body wishing to be more than a bird of passage, more than a seminar sponsor, and sustainably involved in Himalayan environments; might first address itself to some basic questions, as good strategic planners. And then find its best answers. I pose such a helpful approach below

1. *In what specific location* should it begin? The answer it has given itself is the Gangotri area. In these circumstances, I would advise:

a) between the road-head and base camps in the Gangotri area;

b) routes from base camps to higher camps on the main peaks in the area.

2. Who should be the *specific target groups* of its activities? I would suggest:

a) the climbing and trekking community, and the Uttarkashi Institute of Mountaineering;

b) the organisers of expeditions and treks, including tourist and travel agencies;

c) policy makers, e.g. the Indian Mountaineering Foundation (IMF), the Government of India, and the Uttar Pradesh Government.

d) local populations, including pilgrims and their infrastructure.

3. For *what period of time* should one envisage activities for sustainable ecological effect? I would suggest 5 to 10 years, with a review after the 5th and 10th years, against clear sustainability criteria.

4. *What specific programmes and projects?*

a) First, let us begin with target group (c), the policy makers. I would agree, with most of the policy recommendations of the 'Save Gangotri' Action Plan of the 1992 Seminar, around declaring it a National Park; with first priority for hygiene and garbage disposal with about 500,000 pilgrims, besides trekkers and climbers. No hoardings please! Paint ecological wisdom on rocks, Asoka-style. Forest plantations should be by and for local self-managing communities for fuel and fodder, primarily. The choice of plants for local nurseries run by local people as viable propositions should begin with about 5 or 10 species, the choice of local people and foresters. The first saplings may come from forest nurseries to be multiplied by local nurseries. The establishment of local self-managed communities is basic, and should precede any expenditures. Plantings by well-intentioned birds of passage won't endure. This calls for special expertise.

Also on the Policy front the following recommendations:

— dispersal of tourism, trekking and mountaineering; the Himalaya are spacious enough;
— the identification by IMF of suitable forward sites for trekkers and climbers on a viable self-financing basis of chalets with toilets, lights, incinerators for waste disposal, and cooking ranges, run by competent staff, preferably trained local guides;
— appropriate training of, and authority to liaison officers to observe environmental regulations, and to report. Deterrent fines and future disallowance;
— the replication of the unique example of Gandruk Annapurna Conservation area project (Vide p. 82 *The Himalayas, Ecology and Environment*, Vol. 2, 1992-

93); a mix of conservation of local natural resources, community participation, and village houses;*

— expeditions of more than four climbers to bring in their own fuel at and beyond BC. Obligation to take back their own garbage, at least to a retrieval point, from which local authority can dispose it.

b) If HET wishes to put down roots in sustainable eco-development in local villages or a mini-catchment, its emphasis should be on biomass production for fodder and fuel, clean drinking water, wind and solar energy. The latter with the help of suitable Indian and foreign technical agencies. And that will involve years of work, in planning and at the grass-roots.

c) If not the present, putting the next generation at Uttarkashi Mountaineering Institute to school in mountain ecology. How much do we know of the basics of mountain eco-systems, especially forest eco-systems, human settlements, and the eco-systems at and above BC? Concerned as we are with weather, how much do we know of micro-climatic changes in recent decades? We know nothing of the geo-hydrology of mountain springs, which are drying up. Do we know that bird and butterfly watching, over time, can tell us about ecological/climatic changes decades before climatologists? How much do young mountaineers know about the ecology and behaviour of glaciers, their impact on water cycles and climate? Herein lies the journey to self of hardcore mountaineers, who are now developing a conscience about mountain environments. As a guest instructor on mountain ecology on a basic and an advanced course of the Uttarkashi mountain school, I know how such instruction and discussion in the field can be more live, more real, and make mountain training more meaningful than outdoor gymnastics. Mountain life can then become continuous exploration; it can become an internalised experience of high value.

---

* As tourist lodgings, they could be a rich source of income from tourist trekkers.

d) A high-powered HET with internationally famous trustees capable of raising resources, could also sponsor local fact-finding research in the Gangotri area on:

— micro-climatic and ecological changes;
— medium altitude (high temperate) flora and fauna above 2500 m;
— the human impact on the ecology of the Gangotri area beyond Harsil.

5. *What kind of organisation/staff?* This is the last, but a fundamental problem. No organisation can muster all specialisations necessary. I would suggest a Consortium approach of all institutions and persons, Indians and international, who are competent to contribute. HET should be a catalystic learning and action-translating body.

A Local Initiative:
The Sagarmatha Pollution Control Project

MINGMA NORBU SHERPA

Information on the Project and its history was provided by Mingma Norbu Sherpa, Country Representative of the World Wide Fund for Nature (WWF) in Nepal. Extracts are given below.

Summary of the Project

The primary objective of this programme is to provide some immediate solutions, as well as an institutional base, for a long-term commitment to monitoring and alleviating the problems of sanitation, trash disposal and deforestation in Sagarmatha (Everest) National Park.

Sagarmatha National Park, encompassing some 1243 square kilometers in the Eastern Himalaya of Nepal, is home to the world's highest mountain, Everest. In recognition of its spectacular scenery and its unique wildlife and flora, Sagarmatha has the distinction of being a World Heritage Site. Yet it has also earned the title of World's Highest Trash Pit.

An increasingly popular place for both mountain climbers and tourists, the Park was visited by some 15,000 people in 1992. During the climbing season, usually six months of the year, there are often three expeditions at a time at the Everest Base Camp waiting to make an assault on the summit. Some bring with them as much as 10 tons of supplies. Since there is no incentive at present to follow the American mountaineering slogan of "pack out what you bring in," the mountain and entire park area have become a junkyard and health hazard.

Equally grave is the problem of deforestation resulting from both foreign visitors and a burgeoning local population using scarce firewood. The forests of heavily trekked areas in Nepal have been decimated; it is estimated that one mountain climbing expedition can consume up to 40 tons of firewood during its stay in the Park. The resulting shortage of firewood imposes a heavy burden on the local population. And, of course, the ecological consequences can be disastrous.

WWF, in cooperation with His Majesty's Government of Nepal, the Sagarmatha National Park authorities, the local Sherpa community and the Abbot of Tengboche monastery, proposed to launch a public awareness and educational campaign to address these problems along with the long-term trash management field projects to alleviate these problems.

The programme was initially managed by the Sagarmatha Co-operative, composed of members of the National Park Service and the local Sherpa community, and chaired by the Abbot of the Tengboche monastery, who provided the initial impetus for this project. In 1993, the Cooperative has been registered as an NGO by the name of Sagarmatha Pollution Control Committee (SPCC) at the District Administration Office of Solo Khumbu.

Initial funding was utilised to: (1) generate public awareness of the issues, both among the local people and foreign visitors, (2) build an infrastructure for dealing with the biodegradable and non-biodegradable pollutants, (3) provide education and training.

There is also a provision for generating funds for the future continuance of this program through collection of trash deposits and peak fees from the mountaineering and trekking tourism. Recently, under the government policy of ploughing back some portion of the peak fees, Ministry of Tourism and Civil Aviation has been processing to provide some Rs. 3 million (equivalent to US $ 60,000) to the SPCC in order to carry out conservation and development works. WWF Nepal Program has prepared an operational plan for the purpose, and has drafted a Memorandum of Understanding between WWF, HMG and SPCC.

While there have been some attempts to "clean-up" Everest, this is the first programme of its kind that provides the initial funding and professional advice that allows the Nepalese to successfully manage these problems of ecological devastation and degradation.

The Department of National Parks and Wildlife Conservation (DNPWC) in Nepal is committed to upgrading and improving management of the park through development of a management plan, by training personnel and trying to sort out the issues arising from resources used by the local people within the park. However, resources available to the DNPWC to carry out activities to conserve the park are minimal. This programme jointly funded by the WWF and the Ministry of Tourism and Civil Aviation will provide some of those resources.

A Programme Coodinator (a resident of Solo Khumbu) has been hired to coordinate activities in Kathmandu with the Ministry of Tourism and Civil Aviation, Ministry of Forests and Soil Conservation, travel and trekking agencies, international mountaineering communities, and media both in and outside Nepal and the SPCC executing body in the Khumbu. The Program Manager and the Chief Warden of Sagarmatha National Park will implement the programme in close coordination with the people of Khumbu.

The existing mechanism established by the residents of Khumbu will be followed to expand the programme to include other activities such as regular clean up of the mountain itself, provide necessary infrastructure such as trail and bridge repairs, drinking water supplies, improvement of camp sites, and protection of the environment. WWF field office in Kathmandu and the programme coordinator of SPCC will provide both financial and technical support to the executive agency in the Khumbu. A technical advisory body will be sought if necessary in Kathmandu to provide necessary advice to the programme.

Activities to Date

The SPCC executive body based in Namche supervises the project activities and advises the project manager as needed. A General Body Meeting of the SPCC in Namche will meet annually to make recommendations about project activities for pollution control. The advisory committee is composed of lodge owners and operators, local elders, and representatives from high schools, youth clubs, and government agencies operative in the area. World Wide Fund for Nature, the Trekking Agents Association of Nepal, the Nepal Mountaineering Association, the Summiteer's Club of Nepal, the Himalayan Trust, the Ministry of Tourism and Civil Aviation, the Department of National Parks and Wildlife Conservation, and other NGO and government agencies are also represented. The executive committee is composed of the Abbot of Tengboche monastery, the Chief Warden of the Sagarmatha National Park, representatives of the Sagarmatha Club of Namche and of the Himalaya Club of Lukla.

The following is a status report on the activities proposed for immediate action by the executive and advisory committees:

Clean-up Campaign

On July 25, 1991, over 80 local volunteers—including government officials, local leaders, and youth club representatives from several villagers—walked five days to the Everest base camp to start the clean-up campaign. The committee decided that Everest base camp would be the main focus of this clean-up campaign to set the example for future expeditions.

According to Project Manager Ang Phurba Sherpa of Namche, over 500 yak loads (or 30,000 kilograms) of trash that had been left by expedition groups were removed from the base camp alone during the 10-day clean-up period. While cleaning up bottles, cans, plastics and discarded boxes and expedition equipment, the volunteers also found a variety of materials that had been left at higher altitudes and had moved down the mountain as a result of glaciation. The collected garbage was transported by yaks to Gorakhshep, a lower elevation area, where a work force was hired by the project to burn and bury the collected rubbish.

In addition, a mobile team has been formed to make regular rounds of the Gokyo valley, the Everest base camp, and the Nuptse base camp area. The team will monitor the areas to determine whether the expeditions and local lodge owners are maintaining the prescribed sanitation standards.

Establishment of a Deposit System

The project has developed a deposit system that is expected to generate a substantial sum of money to pay for trash removal. The system requires all expedition teams to register, prior to their trek, at Mendalphu where the Park Headquarters of Sagarmatha Park is located. The park collects a deposit of five Nepalese rupees for every kilogram of equipment carried by a team to base camps. The deposits will be returned upon proper disposal of trash at the park headquarters or, at the expense of the expedition, arrangements will be made by the project to clean up the expedition's trash. The specific details of the arrangement are worked out by the warden at Mendalphu.

Public Information Activities

The project has commissioned Wendy Lama of Eco-trekking to write a booklet on mountain manners aimed at educating foreign visitors. Over 50,000 copies of the booklet "Trekking Gently in the Himalaya" have been made available to all trekking and travel agencies to distribute to the tourists. Several articles are also planned for publication in mountain journals and Nepal's newspapers. Finally, NMA and trekking agencies will conduct several workshops a year to raise public awareness of the project's objectives.

Revolving Fund

A revolving fund has been set up at the Rashtriya Banijya Bank in Namche with an initial seed money from WWF (Nepalese Rupees 300,000). This will allow continued funding to cover operational costs of the employees of the cooperative for years to come. The revolving fund is expected to grow as more funds are collected from mountaineering expeditions.

Lodge Owner/Operator Training

The project plans to institute a training programme for lodge owners and operators from Lukla to Lobuche focussing on food preparation, kitchen hygiene, accounting, fuelwood saving technology, and trekker hospitality.

Landfill and Rubbish Collection Points

Landfills and rubbish collection points have been constructed and will be set up at Gorakhshep, Lobuche, Lukla and Namche Bazar. The biggest dump measures 7 m X 7 m, and is 2.5 m deep. Additional sites are planned for Lukla, Phakding, Tengboche, Pheriche, Chukhung, Gokyo, and Dole. The dump sites are being made bird and animal-proof, where possible, through the use of mesh wire and other construction materials.

Latrine Construction

To minimize the solid waste problem, the project is currently building two latrines at Lobuche and one in Gokyo. The nearest lodge owner will be responsible for the daily maintenance of the latrines.

Trash Can Construction

Materials currently are being assembled in Kathmandu and transported to Sagarmatha by porters for trash cans that the project will build. The cans will be distributed, at cost, to interested lodge owners and private home owners. In most locations, trash will be emptied by a paid employee.

Operational Plan

An operational plan for the Sagarmatha Pollution Control Project has been prepared by a team of experts upon consultation with the local people and the concerned government and non-governmental agencies. The plan has identified four major programmes—environment, cultural conservation, tourism development, and community services. Priorities of the Sagarmatha National Park, and the local communities have been listed.

Holding the Himalaya in Trust

CAPT. M.S. KOHLI

Capt. M.S. Kohli, AVSM, FRGS, is Chairman of the Himalayan Environment Trust. He led the successful Indian Expedition to Everest, 1965, and has been on several Himalayan expeditions. He led Air-India's campaign 1971-1989 to popularise trekking in the Himalaya.

He was Vice President and then President of The Indian Mountaineering Foundation for 14 years (1979-1993).

---

* *What do I consider to be the major environmental problems of the Himalaya today?*

These are depletion of forest cover, haphazard construction at many places, particularly on the pilgrim routes, accumulation of rubbish and problems of human waste.

* *How am I and my organisation dealing with questions of garbage, toilets and fuel?*

In regard to garbage, our plan in the enclosed Gangotri Conservation Project are quite clear.

In India where the problem has become much more serious due to large groups of pilgrims, I feel it is necessary to build some rubbish dumps and have a regular rubbish-clearing operation. We have recently installed two toilets in the Himalayan Mountaineering Institute, Darjeeling, where solar heat is used to burn human waste. Only recently in Kathmandu I came across a party which had made an incinerator which can burn plastics and tins. It generates about 1000°C heat by burning the disposable portion of the garbage. It is still in the development stage and we have yet to carry out a proper experiment. We also need to build a number of micro hydro-generators as well as to make available stocks of LPG and kerosene oil as alternate sources of energy. I am not very sure about the effective utilisation of solar heat but possibly at some places it can be tried.

* *What practical measures are suggested to deal with these problems?*

I feel some of the ideas utilised in the Annapurna Conservation Area Project are good. The support of the local population of the Himalayan area is a must, and we in the Trust are very keen to ensure local participation in our Himalayan Environmental projects. Some details mentioned in the Gangotri Conservation Project report may be worth considering.

The Gangotri Conservation Project

Sushil Gupta is Director of the Gangotri Conservation Project; he has trekked extensively in Garhwal and visited Tibet. He is the Managing Director (Finance and Marketing) of Asian Hotels Ltd., Treasurer of the Federation of Hotels and Restaurants of Northern India, and a member of the Advisory Board, Institute of Vocational Studies, Himachal Pradesh University. Through the Rotary Club, he undertook the rehabilitation of a village in Uttarkashi which was destroyed by the earthquake of 1991.

The Gangotri basin, of all degraded areas, is one of the most polluted areas in the Himalaya. Besides 75 mountaineering expeditions and nearly 25,000 trekkers, this area is visited by nearly 250,000 pilgrims annually, which adds a new dimension to the problems in the Indian Himalaya. Large stretches of forest cover have been destroyed. There are over 50 tonnes of rubbish lying on and around the trail leading to the source of the Ganges and beyond, at the base camps of several high mountains which ring the sacred area. The situation is alarming, and of serious concern not only to Indians, being the source of India's most sacred river, but to Himalayan lovers all over the world. The Ganges, for centuries, has been a part of India's culture and civilisation. While a massive project has been launched by the Ministry of Environment and Forests of the Govt. of India, to clean up the Ganges, it is equally important to ensure the sanctity of the source of the Ganges and the surrounding areas. Unrestricted construction has played havoc with its ecology. It is not possible to restrict the visitors to the sacred

106

area which many a devout Hindu cherish a life-long ambition to visit. At the same time, it is important to ensure the pristine glory of this area and to lay strict norms to avoid any further destruction of forest, reaccumulation of rubbish and reckless construction.

Himalayan Environment Trust

The Himalayan Environment Trust (HET) was set up on 14 October 1989 by some of the leading mountaineers of the world to mobilise the support from mountaineers, trekkers, Alpine Clubs, adventure tour operators, and the Himalayan region governments, to protect the Himalayan environment, its flora, fauna and natural resources, as well as to protect the customs and interest of the local people; to evolve a code of conduct and ethics to be followed by all visitors to the Himalayan region, as part of a continuing effort to maintain and sustain the well-being of the Himalayan environment; to hold international conferences, seminars, and Himalayan tourism meets, to discuss problems of the Himalayan environment and focus world attention on such matters.

The Board of Trustees consists of Sir Edmund Hillary, KBE (Patron); Capt. M.S. Kohli, AVSM, FRGS (Chairman); Richard Blum; Chris Bonington, CBE; Maurice Herzog; Reinhold Messner and Junko Tabei.

The Board of Trustees decided to mount a major Himalayan Environment Trek to Gangotri from June 18-26, 1994 consisting of about 100 enthusiasts from all over the world. The trek will be led by Reinhold Messner, a Trustee of HET, and the first man in the world to climb all the fourteen 8000 m Himalayan peaks and Mount Everest solo without oxygen.

Sonia Gandhi, Chairperson of the Rajiv Gandhi Foundation, has been requested to flag-off the team in Delhi at 7.30 A.M. on June 19, 1994. On the return of the trekking team, a major Environment Conference is being organised at Mussoorie on June 27-28 to which the Ministers of Environment from all the Himalayan countries are being invited to discuss and finalise Government's/ People's Action towards the preservation of the Himalayas. Other Trustees of the HET will also participate.

Gangotri Conservation Project

Gangotri Conservation Project (GCP) is an innovative new plan to protect this remarkable area from further degradation. It evolves a brand new concept in protected-area management, evolving land use method of resource management, traditional subsistence activities and alternative energy projects to minimise the impact of tourists and pilgrims, and upgrade the local standard of living.

The Project will have a grassroots philosophy in all aspects of conservation and development process. By giving certain power to the local people with proper skill and technical knowledge and financial assistance, GCP plans to conserve this sacred area, and improve the quality of life of the local people. Some of the activities of the Project will include forest conservation, encouraging alternative sources of energy, conservation education, starting visitors' awareness programmes and highlighting sustainable community development.

GCP Objectives

a) To remove the present rubbish beyond Uttarkashi in the Gangotri basin.
b) To take all possible steps to reduce accumulation of future rubbish.
c) Intensive afforestation in the area, and to reduce use of wood by introduction of alternative sources of energy such as solar cookers, solar heaters and micro hydro-electric projects, and arranging supplies of LPG/kerosene oil.
d) Building toilets.
e) Enforcement of legislation regarding new construction in the area.
f) To interact with packaging firms and research organisations to evolve bio-degradable packaging for use by all visitors to the Himalaya including pilgrims.

Action Plan

a) To remove the present rubbish in the area it is proposed to secure the help of the army, ITBP, NCC, students from local schools, Indian Mountaineering Foundation, Nehru Institute of Mountaineering, Uttarkashi, Garhwal Vikas Mandal and the District Magistrate, Uttarkashi.

b) *Other Steps*
    i) hoardings
    ii) leaflets
    iii) rubbish dumps and their disposal mechanism
    iv) adequate supply of LPG and kerosene oil, especially during the pilgrimage season.
    v) selection of suitable toilets and their upkeep
    vi) formulation of regulations and guidelines
    vii) viability of micro hydel-project (100 to 1000 KVA capacity).

Afforestation

To utilise Army/ITBP, NCC, hill schools, IMF and the Department of Forests.

Tentative Organisation

An autonomous committee will oversee the project and will be managed by the Director GCP, assisted by Jt. Director and Director, HET, with a help of full time staff consisting of GCP Chief Warden, three wardens, and a 10 member rubbish-cleaning squad.

The GCP will be launched by the Hon'ble Chief Minister of U.P. Govt. at Mussoorie on June 27-28, 1994.

The Himalayan Code of Conduct

The International Union of Alpinist Associations (UIAA) has adopted the following code of conduct which has also been issued by the Himalayan Environment Trust.

By following these simple guidelines, you can help preserve the unique environment and ancient cultures of the Himalaya.

Protect the Natural Environment

* *Campsite*: Remember that another party will be using the same campsite after you have vacated it. Therefore, leave the campsite cleaner than you found it.

* *Limit deforestation*: Make no open fires and discourage others from doing so on your behalf. Where water is heated by scarce firewood, use as little as possible. When possible choose accommodation that uses kerosene or fuel-efficient fire-wood stoves. You will help the cause greatly by taking with you some saplings and planting these on your trail.

* *In a safe place burn dry paper and packets*: bury other waste paper and biodegradable material including food. Carry back all non-biodegradable litter. If you come across other peoples' rubbish, remove their rubbish as well.

* *Keep local water clean and avoid using pollutants* such as detergents in streams or springs. If no toilet facilities are available, make sure you are at least 30 metres away from water sources, and bury or cover wastes.

* *Plants should be left to flourish in their natural environment*—taking cuttings seeds and roots is illegal in many parts of the Himalaya.

* *Help your guides and porters to follow conservation measures*—do not allow the cooks or porters to throw garbage in the nearby stream or river.

* *When taking photographs, respect privacy*—ask permission and use restraint.

* *Respect holy places*—preserve what you have come to see, never touch or remove religious objects. Remove shoes when visiting temples.

* *Refrain from giving money to children since it will encourage begging*—a donation to a project, health centre or school is a more constructive way to help.

* *Respect for local etiquette earns you respect*—loose, lightweight clothes are preferable to revealing shorts, skimpy tops and tight fitting action wear. Hand holding or kissing in public are disapproved by local people.

Respect local traditions, protect local cultures, maintain local pride.
The Himalaya may change you—please do not change them.

Index

Prepared by Kaivan Mistry